D0353324

TURKISH

Phrase Book
&Dictionary

Figen Sat Yilmaz

BBC Active, an imprint of Educational Publishers LLP, part of the Pearson Education Group, Edinburgh Gate, Harlow, Essex CM20 2JE, England

First published 2007.

ISBN 978-1-4066-1213-4

Cover design: Two Associates
Cover photograph: AA World Travel Library/Alamy
Insides design: Pentacor book design
Layout: Pryor Design
Illustrations © Joanna Kerr, New Division
Development manager: Tara Dempsey
Series editor: Philippa Goodrich
Senior production controller: Man Fai Lau

Printed and bound in China. CTPSC/01

The Publisher's policy is to use paper manufactured from sustainable forests.

how to use this book

This book is divided into colour-coded sections to help you find the language you need as quickly as possible. You can also refer to the **contents** on pages 4–5, and the contents lists at the start of each section.

Along with travel and language tips, each section contains:

 YOU MAY WANT TO SAY...
language you'll need for every situation

 YOU MAY SEE...
words and phrases you'll see on signs or in print

 YOU MAY HEAR... questions, instructions or information people may ask or give you

On page 12 you'll find **essentials**, a list of basic, all-purpose phrases to help you start communicating straight away.

Many of the phrases can be adapted by simply using another word from the dictionary. For instance, take the question Havaalanı nerede? (Where is the airport?), if you want to know where the *station* is, just substitute istasyon (station) for havaalanı to give İstasyon nerede?

The **pronunciation guide** is based on English sounds, and is explained on page 6. If you want some guidance on how the Turkish language works, see **basic grammar** on page 159.

The **dictionary** is separated into two sections: English–Turkish (page 169) and Turkish–English (page 203).

We welcome any comments or suggestions about this book, but in the meantime, have a good trip – İyi yolculuklar!

contents

pronunciation guide

Turkish pronunciation is very regular – you can tell how a word is pronounced from the way it is written, once you know what each sound represents. In Turkish every letter is pronounced fully and clearly, with each letter usually representing a single sound.

Turkish words carry only a very light stress, generally on the last syllable. On the whole though, stresses are hardly noticeable when strung together in words and phrases, so are not shown in this book.

✳ vowels

The majority of Turkish vowels are short, except as described below. In the pronunciation guide a long vowel is shown by a colon (:) placed after it.

If a vowel is followed by ğ, it is pronounced long, and there is no 'g' sound, e.g:

oğul *o:ul* (son)	doğu *do:u* (east)
öğle *ö:le* (noon)	dağ *da:* (mountain)

Some words borrowed from other languages (especially Arabic and Persian) have kept their long vowels in Turkish, e.g:

lazım *la:zuhm* (necessary)   dahil *da:hil* (included)

LETTER	APPROX ENGLISH EQUIVALENT	SHOWN IN BOOK AS	EXAMPLE	PRONOUNCED AS
a	between **u** in 'bus' and **a** in 'cat'	a	baba	*baba*
e	**e** in 'bed'	e	et	*et*
ı	**e** in 'the cat'	uh	ılık	*uhluhk*
i	between **i** in 'bit' and **ee** in 'meet'	i	iki	*iki*
o	**o** in 'hot'	o	ok	*ok*
ö	**o** in 'word' or **i** in 'bird'	ö	örnek	*örnek*
u	between **u** in 'put' or **oo** in 'foot'	u	uzun	*uzun*
ü	between **oo** in 'too' or **ew** in 'new'	ew	üzüm	*ewzewm*

✳ consonants

Most Turkish consonants are pronounced in much the same way as in English. If there is a consonant combination or double consonant, both letters are pronounced. English speakers especially should be careful about the separate pronunciation of the consonant combinations ph, sh, and th. For example, ph in kütüphahe (library) is pronounced like the 'ph' in 'uphill'; sh in ishal (diarrhoea) like the 'sh' in 'glasshouse'; and 'th' in ithal (imported) like the 'th' in 'cathouse'.

LETTER	APPROX ENGLISH EQUIVALENT	SHOWN IN BOOK AS	EXAMPLE	PRONOUNCED AS
b	**b** in 'but'	b	bebek	*bebek*
c	**j** in 'jam'	j	cam	*jam*
ç	**ch** in 'chair'	ch	çanta	*chanta*
d	**d** in 'door'	d	doktor	*doktor*
f	**f** in 'feet'	f	fakat	*fakat*
g	**g** in 'go'	g	gece	*geje*
ğ	not pronounced, but lengthens the preceding vowel	:	bağ	*ba:*
h	**h** in 'hot'	h	hava	*hava*
j	**s** in 'leisure'	zh	ruj	*ruzh*
k	**k** in 'keep'	k	kapı	*kapuh*
l	**l** in 'lift'	l	bil	*bil*
m	**m** in 'milk'	m	masa	*masa*
n	**n** in 'no'	n	ne	*ne*
p	**p** in 'pool'	p	para	*para*
r	rolled at back of mouth	r	kuru	*kuru*
s	**s** in 'sea'	s	sarı	*saruh*
ş	**sh** in 'ship'	sh	kiş	*kuhsh*
t	**t** in 'tea'	t	Türkçe	*tewrkche*
v	**v** in 'very'	v	ve	*ve*
y	**y** in 'yes'	y	yıl	*yuhl*
z	**z** in 'zoo'	z	zor	*zor*

✳ the Turkish alphabet

There are 29 letters in the Turkish alphabet. The pronunciation of each is given below, in case you need to spell out an address or place name. Note that 'q', 'w', and 'x' do not exist in Turkish. Proper nouns (names) take an apostrophe before an ending is added, e.g:

Ankara'da *ankarada* (in Ankara)
Ayşe'ye *aysheye* (to Ayşe)

LETTER	PRONOUNCED
A a	*a*
B, b	*be*
C, c	*je*
Ç, ç	*che*
D, d	*de*
E, e	*e*
F, f	*fe*
G, g	*ge*
Ğ, ğ	*yumushak ge*
H, h	*he*
I, ı	*uh*
İ, i	*ee*
J, j	*zhe*
K, k	*ke*
L, l	*le*

LETTER	PRONOUNCED
M, m	*me*
N, n	*ne*
O, o	*o*
Ö, ö	*ö*
P, p	*pe*
R, r	*re*
S, s	*se*
Ş, ş	*she*
T, t	*te*
U, u	*oo*
Ü, ü	*ew*
V, v	*ve*
Y, y	*ye*
Z, z	*ze*

the basics

*essentials

English	Turkish	Pronunciation
Hello.	Merhaba.	*merhaba*
Goodbye.	Güle güle.	*gewle gewle*
Good morning.	Günaydın.	*gewnayduhn*
Good evening.	İyi akşamlar.	*iyi akshamlar*
Good night.	İyi geceler.	*iyi gejeler*
Yes.	Evet.	*evet*
No.	Hayır.	*hayuhr*
Please.	Lütfen.	*lewtfen*
Thank you (very much).	(çok) Teşekkür ederim.	*(chok) teshekkewr ederim*
You're welcome./ Don't mention it.	Bir şey değil.	*bir shey de:il*
I don't know.	Bilmiyorum.	*bilmiyorum*
I don't understand.	Anlamıyorum.	*anlamuhyorum*
I only speak a little bit of Turkish.	Çok az Türkçe biliyorum.	*chok az tewrkche biliyorum*
Do you speak English?	İngilizce biliyor musunuz?	*ingilizje biliyor musunuz*
Is there anyone who speaks English?	İngilizce bilen birisi var mı?	*ingilizje bilen birisi varmuh*
Pardon?	Affedersiniz?	*affedersiniz*
Could you repeat that please?	Tekrar söyler misiniz lütfen?	*tekrar söyler misiniz lewtfen*
More slowly, please.	Daha yavaş lütfen.	*daha yavash lewtfen*

How do you say it in Turkish?	Türkçe de nasıl söylersiniz?	*tewrkchede nasuhl söylersiniz*
Excuse me./Sorry.	Affedersiniz.	*affedersiniz*
I'm sorry.	Özür dilerim.	*özewr dilerim*
Unfortunately...	Maalesef...	*maalesef...*
OK, fine./That's all right.	Tamam/Oldu.	*tamam/oldu*
Cheers!	Şerefe!	*sherefe*
I'd like...	...istiyorum.	*...istiyorum*
Is there (any)...?	...var mı?	*...varmuh*
Are there (any)...?	...var mı?	*...varmuh*
Do you have...?	...var mı?	*...varmuh*
What's this?	Bu nedir?	*bu nedir*
How much is it?	ne kadar?/kaç lira?	*ne kadar/kach lira*
What time...?	...saat kaçta?	*...saat kachta*
Where is/are...?	...nerede?	*...nerede*
How do I/we get to...?	...nasıl giderim?	*...nasuhl giderim*
Can you...		
tell me...?	...söyler misiniz?	*...söyler misiniz*
give me...?	...verir misiniz?	*...verir misiniz*
show me on the map?	haritada gösterir misiniz?	*haritada gösterir misiniz*
write it down?	Yazar mısınız?	*yazar muhsuhnuhz*
Help!	İmdat!	*imdat*

✳ numbers

1	bir	*bir*
2	iki	*iki*
3	üç	*ewch*
4	dört	*dört*
5	beş	*besh*
6	altı	*altuh*
7	yedi	*yedi*
8	sekiz	*sekiz*
9	dokuz	*dokuz*
10	on	*on*
11	on bir	*on bir*
12	on iki	*on iki*
13	on üç	*on ewch*
14	on dört	*on dört*
15	on beş	*on besh*
16	on altı	*on altuh*
17	on yedi	*on yedi*
18	on sekiz	*on sekiz*
19	on dokuz	*on dokuz*
20	yirmi	*yirmi*
21	yirmi bir	*yirmi bir*
22...	yirmi iki	*yirmi iki*
30	otuz	*otuz*
31	otuz bir	*otuz bir*
32...	otuz iki	*otuz iki*
40	kırk	*kuhrk*
50	elli	*elli*
60	altmış	*altmuhsh*
70	yetmiş	*yetmish*
80	seksen	*seksen*
90	doksan	*doksan*
100	yüz	*yewz*
101	yüz bir	*yewz bir*

102...	yüz iki	*yewz iki*
200	iki yüz	*iki yewz*
250	iki yüz elli	*iki yewz elli*
300	üç yüz	*ewch yewz*
400	dört yüz	*dört yewz*
500	beş yüz	*besh yewz*
600	altı yüz	*altuh yewz*
700	yedi yüz	*yedi yewz*
800	sekiz yüz	*sekiz yewz*
900	dokuz yüz	*dokuz yewz*
1,000	bin	*bin*
2,000	iki bin	*iki bin*
3,000	üç bin	*ewch bin*
4,000	dört bin	*dört bin*
5,000	beş bin	*besh bin*
100,000	yüz bin	*yewz bin*
one million	bir milyon	*bir milyon*
one and a half million	bir buçuk milyon	*bir buchuk milyon*

✻ ordinal numbers

first	birinci	*birinji*
second	ikinci	*ikinji*
third	üçüncü	*ewchewnjew*
fourth	dördüncü	*dördewnjew*
fifth	beşinci	*beshinji*
sixth	altıncı	*altuhnjuh*
seventh	yedinci	*yedinji*
eighth	sekizinci	*sekizinji*
ninth	dokuzuncu	*dokuzunju*
tenth	onuncu	*onunju*

✳ fractions

a quarter	çeyrek	*cheyrek*
a half (when you use it with a number)	buçuk	*buchuk*
(when you use it alone)	yarım	*yaruhm*
three-quarters	üç-çeyrek	*üch-cheyrek*
a third	üçte bir	*üchte bir*
two-thirds	üçte iki	*üchte iki*

✳ days

Monday	Pazartesi	*pazartesi*
Tuesday	Salı	*saluh*
Wednesday	Çarşamba	*charshamba*
Thursday	Perşembe	*pershembe*
Friday	Cuma	*juma*
Saturday	Cumartesi	*jumartesi*
Sunday	Pazar	*Pazar*

✳ months

January	Ocak	*ojak*
February	Şubat	*shubat*
March	Mart	*mart*
April	Nisan	*nisan*
May	Mayıs	*mayuhs*
June	Haziran	*haziran*

the basics

16

July	Temmuz	*temmuz*
August	Ağustos	*a:ustos*
September	Eylül	*eylewl*
October	Ekim	*ekim*
November	Kasım	*kasuhm*
December	Aralık	*araluhk*

✳ seasons

spring	İlkbahar	*Ilkbahar*
summer	Yaz	*yaz*
autumn	Sonbahar	*sonbahar*
winter	Kış	*kuhsh*

✳ dates

What day is it today?	Bugün günlerden ne?	*bugewn gewnlerden ne*
What date is it today?	Bugün ayın kaçı?	*bugewn ayuhn kachuh*
When is... your birthday?	...ne zaman? Doğum gününüz	*...ne zaman do:um gewnewnewz*
(It's) the fifteenth of April.	Nisan'ın on beşi.	*nisanuhn on beshi*
On the fifteenth of April.	On beş Nisan'da.	*on besh nisanda*

the basics

17

✻ telling the time

● Turkey uses both the 12-hour and 24-hour clocks. The 24-hour clock is the more formal system used mainly for written schedules. It is easy to tell the time if it is on the hour or half past. To say 'It's... o'clock.' you say saat (hour) and the number, e.g. saat yedi (It's seven o'clock). For 'half past' add buçuk, e.g. saat yedi buçuk (It's half past seven). For times past the hour, the numbers indicating the hour have the endings -ı, -i,-u,-ü, and geçiyor is used, e.g. Saat üçü on geçiyor (It's ten past three). The endings -e,-a, which are attached to the number indicating the hour, are used with var to say 'to the hour', e.g. Saat üçe on var. (It's ten to three.)

● To say 'at...' you add one of the endings -de,-da,-te,-ta to the number if it is 'on the hour' or 'half past', e.g. saat üçte (at three o'clock), saat üç buçukta (at half past three). To say 'at.... past the hour' use geçe, e.g. beşi yirmi geçe (at twenty past five), to say 'at...to the hour' use kala, e.g. beşe yirmi kala (at twenty to five).

YOU MAY WANT TO SAY...

● **What time is it?**	Saat kaç?	*saat kach*
● **What time does it...**	Saat kaçta...	*saat kachta...*
open?/close?	açılıyor?/kapanıyor?	*achuhluhyor/kapanuhyor*
start?/finish?	başlıyor?/bitiyor?	*bashluhyor/bitiyor*

- It's...

10 o'clock	Saat on	saat on
half past ten	Saat on buçuk	saat on buchuk
twenty past five	Saat beşi yirmi geçiyor	saat beshi yirmi gechiyor
twenty to five	Saat beşe yirmi var	saat beshe yirmi var
a quarter past...	...çeyrek geçiyor	...cheyrek gechiyor
a quarter to...	...çeyrek var	...cheyrek var
midday	Öğle	ö:le
half past twelve	Yarım	yaruhm
midnight	Gece yarısı	geje yaruhsuh

- At...

a quarter past nine	Dokuzu çeyrek geçe	dokuzu cheyrek geche
a quarter to ten	Ona çeyrek kala	ona cheyrek kala
twenty past ten	Onu yirmi geçe	onu yirmi geche
twenty-five to ten	Ona yirmi beş kala	ona yirmi besh kala
half past ten	On buçuk	on buchuk

- In...

ten minutes	On dakika	on dakika
half an hour	Yarım saat içinde	yaruhm saat ichinde
an hour	Bir saat	bir saat

	...içinde	...ichinde

✱ time phrases

YOU MAY WANT TO SAY...

● day	gün	gewn
● week	hafta	hafta
● fortnight	iki hafta/on beş gün	iki hafta/on besh gewn

● **month**	ay	*ay*
● **year**	yıl/sene	*yuhl/sene*
● **today**	bugün	*bugewn*
● **tomorrow**	yarın	*yaruhn*
● **the day after tomorrow**	ertesi gün	*ertesi gewn*
● **yesterday**	dün	*dewn*
● **the day before yesterday**	evvelsi gün	*evvelsi gewn*
● **this morning**	bu sabah	*bu sabah*
this afternoon	bu öğleden sona	*bu ö:leden sonra*
this evening	bu akşam	*bu aksham*
tonight	bu gece	*bu geje*
● **on Friday**	Cuma günü	*juma gewnew*
on Fridays	Cumaları	*jumalaruh*
● **every...**	her...	*her...*
Friday	Cuma	*juma*
week	hafta	*hafta*
● **for...**	...-dır./ ...-dür.	*...-duhr/...-dewr*
a week/a day	bir hafta/Bir gün	*bir hafta/bir gewn*
two weeks/two days	iki hafta/İki gün	*iki hafta/iki gewn*
two years	iki yıl	*iki yuhl*
a month	bir ay	*bir ay*
● **I'm here for two weeks.**	İki haftadır buradayım.	*iki haftaduhr buradayuhm*
● **I've been here for a month.**	Bir aydır buradayım.	*bir ayduhr buradayuhm*

- I've been learning Turkish for two years. | İki yıldır Türkçe öğreniyorum. | *iki yuhlduhr tewrkche ö:reniyorum*

- next... | gelecek... | *gelejek...*
  - Tuesday | Salı | *saluh*
  - week | hafta | *hafta*

- last... | geçen... | *gechen...*
  - week | hafta | *hafta*

- last night | dün gece | *dewn geje*

- a week ago | bir hafta önce | *bir hafta önje*

- a year ago | bir yıl/sene önce | *bir yuhl/sene önje*

- since... | ...-den/-dan beri | *...-den/-dan beri*
  - yesterday | dün | *dewn*
  - last week | geçen hafta | *gechen hafta*

- It's... | |
  - early | erken | *erken*
  - late | geç | *gech*

* measurements

MEASUREMENTS		
centimetre	santimetre	*santimetre*
metre	metre	*metre*
kilometre	kilometre	*kilometre*
mile	mil	*mil*
a litre	bir litre	*bir litre*
25 litres	yirmi beş litre	*yirmi besh litre*
gramme	gram	*gram*

the basics

21

100 grammes	yüz gram	*yewz gram*
200 grammes	iki yüz gram	*iki yewz gram*
kilo(s)	kilo/kilogram	*kilo/kilogram*

CONVERSIONS

1km = *0.62 miles*	200g = *7oz*
1 mile = *1.61 km*	¼1b = *113g*
1 litre = *1.8 pints*	½ kilo = *1.1lb*
100g = *3.5oz*	½lb = *225g*
1oz = *28g*	1 kilo = *2.2lb*
1lb = *450g*	

To convert kilometres to miles, divide by 8 and multiply by 5 e.g. 16 kilometres (16/8 = 2, 2x5 = 10) = 10 miles.

For miles to kilometres: divide by 5 and multiply by 8 e.g. 50 miles (50/5 = 10, 10x8 = 80) = 80 kilometres.

✳ clothes and shoe sizes

women's clothes

UK	8	10	12	14	16	18	20
Continent	36	38	40	42	44	46	48

men's clothes

UK	36	38	40	42	44	46	48
Continent	46	48	50	52	54	56	58

men's shirts

UK	14	14½	15	15½	16	16½	17
Continent	36	37	38	39	41	42	43

shoes

UK	2	3	4	5	6	7	8	9	10	11
Continent	35	36	37	38	39	40	41	42	43	44

✳ national holidays and festivals

● There are two important Muslim religious festivals, the dates of which change according to the Muslim Lunar Calendar. Şeker/Ramazan Bayramı –*sheker/ramazan bayramuh* (Eid-ul-Fitr) marks the end of the Islamic month of Ramadan, and lasts for three days. Kurban bayramı –*kurban bayramuh* (Eid-ul-Adha) occurs two months and ten days after the Şeker Bayramı, and lasts for four days.

Yılbaşı	*yuhlbashuh*	**New Year's Day**
Çocuk Bayramı	*chojuk bayramuh*	**Children's Day: 23 April**
Gençlik ve Spor Bayramı	*genchlik ve spor bayramuh*	**Youth and Sports Day: 19 May**

national holidays and festivals

Zafer Bayramı	*zafer bayramuh*	**Victory Day: 30 August**
Cumhuriyet Bayramı	*jumhuriyet bayramuh*	**Republic Day: 29 October**

general conversation

* greetings

● The word **merhaba** is an all-purpose informal greeting that means 'hello'. In rural areas you will hear the more traditional religious greeting **Selaymünaleykum** (Peace be with you). The response is **Aleykumselam** (Peace be with you too).

● There are two ways of saying 'you' - **sen** (singular/informal) and **siz** (plural/formal). The endings on the verbs change depending on whether you are addressing someone as **sen** or **siz**. We have generally used the formal form in this book.

● When introducing or addressing people formally, you put **Bey** (for men) and **Hanım** (for women) after their first names, e.g. **Ahmet Bey** or **Ayşe Hanım**. To be more formal, you put **Sayın** (both for men and women) before the surname, e.g. **Sayın Kaya**, **Sayın Özdemir**. Alternatively you can put **Bay** (for men) or **Bayan** (for women) before the surnames, e.g. **Bay Kaya**, **Bayan Özdemir**, which is like saying Mr Kaya or Ms Özdemir.

YOU MAY WANT TO SAY...

● **Hello.**	Merhaba.	*Merhaba*
● **Good morning.**	Günaydın.	*gewnayduhn*
● **Good day.**	İyi günler.	*iyi gewnler*
● **Good evening.**	İyi akşamlar.	*iyi akshamlar*

general conversation

Good night.	İyi geceler.	*iyi gejeler*
Goodbye. (if you are leaving)	Allahaısmarladık.	*ala:smalaladuhk*
Goodbye. (if you are staying behind)	Güle güle.	*gewle gewle*
See you later.	Görüşmek üzere.	*görewshmek ewzere*
How are you?		
(formal)	Nasılsın?	*nasuhlsuhn*
(informal)	Nasılsınız?	*nasuhlsuhnuhz*
How are things?	Nasıl gidiyor?	*nasuhl gidiyor*
Fine, thanks.	İyiyim, teşekkür ederim.	*iyiyim, teshekkewr ederim.*
And you?		
(singular/informal)	Ya sen?	*ya sen*
(plural/formal)	Ya siz?	*ya siz*

✳ introductions

YOU MAY WANT TO SAY...

My name is... (man)	İsmim...	*ismim...*
This is... (referring to a man)		
Mr Brown	Bay Brown	*bay brown*
my husband	Eşim	*eshim*
my son	Oğlum	*o:lum*
my boyfriend/ fiancé	Erkek arkadaşım/ nişanlım	*erkek arkadashuhm/ nishanluhm*
my friend	Arkadaşım	*arkadashuhm*

talking about yourself

- **This is...** (referring to a woman)
  - **Miss/Mrs Brown** — Bayan Brown — *bayan brown*
  - **my wife** — Eşim — *eshim*
  - **my daughter** — Kızım — *kuhzuhm*
  - **my girlfriend/ fiancée** — Kız arkadaşım/ nişanlım — *kuhz arkadashuhm/ nishanluhm*
  - **my friend** — Arkadaşım — *arkadashuhm*

- **Pleased to meet you.** — Memnun oldum. — *memnun oldum*

✳ talking about yourself

- **I'm...** — Ben... — *ben...*
  - **English** — İngilizim — *ingilizim*
  - **Scottish** — İskoçyalıyım — *iskochyaluhyuhm*
  - **Irish** — İrlandalıyım — *irlandaluhyuhm*
  - **Welsh** — Galliyim — *galliyim*

- **I/We live in...** — ... oturuyorum/ oturuyoruz. — *... oturuyorum/ oturuyoruz*
  - **London** — Londra'da — *londrada*
  - **Edinburgh** — Edinburgh'da — *edinburghda*

- **I'm... years old.** — Ben... yaşındayım. — *ben... yashuhndayuhm*

- **He's/she's five years old.** — O beş yaşında. — *o besh yashuhnda*

- **I'm a...** — Ben... — *ben...*
  - **nurse** — hemşireyim — *hemshireyim*
  - **student** — öğrenciyim — *ö:renjiyim*

I work in/for...	... çalışıyorum.	*...chaluhshuhyorum*
a bank	Bir bankada	*bir bankada*
a computer	Bir bilgisayar	*bir bilgisayar*
firm	firmasında	*firmasuhnda*
I'm unemployed.	İşsizim.	*ishsizim*
I'm self-	Kendi işimde	*kendi ishimde*
employed.	çalışıyorum.	*chaluhshuhyorum*
I'm...	Ben...	*ben...*
married	evliyim	*evliyim*
divorced	eşimden	*eshimden*
	boşandım	*boshanduhm*
separated	eşimden ayrıldım	*eshimden*
		ayruhlduhm
single	bekarım	*bekaruhm*
a widower/	dulum	*dulum*
widow		
I have...	...var.	*...var*
three children	Üç çocuğum	*ewch choju:um*
one brother	Bir erkek kardeşim	*bir erkek kardeshim*
I don't have...	...yok.	*...yok*
any children	Hiç çocuğum	*hich choju:um*
any brothers or	Hiç kardeşim	*hich kardeshim*
sisters		
I'm on holiday here.	Burada tatildeyim.	*burada tatildeyim*
I'm here on	İş için buradayım.	*ish ichin buradayuhm*
business.		
I'm here with my...	Ben burada...	*ben burada...*
family	ailemleyim	*ailemleyim*
colleague	iş arkadaşımlayım	*ish*
		arkadashuhmlayuhm

general conversation

29

My husband/wife works in...	Eşim...-de/da/te/ta çalışıyor.	*eshim...-de/da/te/ta chaluhshuhyor.*
I speak very little Turkish.	Çok az Türkçe konuşuyorum.	*chok az tewrkche konushuyorum.*

✳ asking about other people

YOU MAY WANT TO SAY...

Where do you come from?	Nerelisiniz?	*nerelisiniz*
What's your name?	İsminiz ne?	*isminiz ne*
Are you married?	Evli misiniz?	*evli misiniz*
Do you have...	...var mı?	*...varmuh*
any children?	Çocuklarınız	*chojuklaruhnuhz*
any brothers and sisters?	Kardeşleriniz	*kardeshleriniz*
a girlfriend?	Kız arkadaşınız	*kuhz arkadashuhnuhz*
a boyfriend?	Erkek arkadaşınız	*erkek arkadashuhnuhz*
How old are you/they?	Kaç yaşındasınız/ yaşındalar?	*kach yashuhndasuhnuhz/ yashuhndalar*
Is this your...	Bu...	*bu...*
husband/wife?	eşiniz mi?	*eshinizmi*
friend (m/f)?	arkadaşınız mı?	*arkadashuhnuhzmuh*

general conversation

● Where are you going?	Nereye gidiyorsunuz?	*nereye gidiyorsunuz*
● Where are you staying?	Nerede kalıyorsunuz?	*nerede kaluhyorsunuz*
● Where do you live?	Nerede oturuyorsunuz?	*nerede oturuyorsunuz*
● What do you do?	Ne yapıyorsunuz?	*ne yapuhyorsunuz*
● What are you studying?	Ne okuyorsunuz?	*ne okuyorsunuz*

✳ chatting

● Istanbul is very beautiful.	İstanbul çok güzel.	*istanbul chok gewzel*
● I like Istanbul (very much).	İstanbul'u (çok) seviyorum.	*istanbulu (chok) seviyorum*
● It's the first time I've been to Istanbul.	İstanbul'a ilk defa geliyorum.	*istanbula ilk defa geliyorum*
● I come to Istanbul often.	İstanbul'a sık sık gelirim.	*istanbula suhk suhk gelirim*
● Are you from here?	Buralı mısınız?	*buraluh muhsuhnuhz*
● Have you ever been to... Kemer?	...hiç gittiniz mi? Kemer'e	*...hich gittinizmi* *kemere*
● Did you like it?	Sevdiniz mi?	*sevdinizmi*

the weather

YOU MAY HEAR...

İstanbul'u seviyor musunuz?	*istanbulu seviyor musunuz*	Do you like Istanbul?
Kaş'a hiç gittiniz mi?	*kasha hich gittinizmi*	Have you been to Kaş before?
Ne zamana kadar buradasınız?	*ne zamana kadar buradasuhnuhz*	When are you here until?
Çok güzel Türkçe konuşuyorsunuz.	*chok gewze tewrkche konushuyorsunuz*	You speak Turkish very well..
...hakkında ne düşünüyorsunuz?	*...hakkuhnda ne dewshewnewyorsunuz*	What do you think of...?

✳ the weather

YOU MAY WANT TO SAY...

It's a beautiful day!	Güzel bir gün!	*gewzel bir gewn*
What fantastic weather!	Hava ne kadar güzel!	*hava ne kadar gewzel*
It's (very)...	Çok...	*chok...*
hot	sıcak	*suhcak*
cold	soğuk	*so:uk*
windy	rüzgarlı	*rewzgarluh*
What's the forecast?	Hava durumu nasıl	*hava durumu nasıl*
It's...	...yağıyor.	*...ya:uhyor*
raining	Yağmur	*ya:mur*
snowing	Kar	*kar*

✳ likes and dislikes

- I like... (sing.)
  football
  dogs

  ... seviyorum.
  Futbol
  köpek

  ... seviyorum
  futbol
  köpek

- I love...

  ...-(y)ı/i/u/ü çok
  seviyorum.

  ...(y)uh/i/u/ew chok
  seviyorum

  the beach
  bananas

  Sahil
  Muz

  sa:hil
  muz

- I don't like...
  the rain
  tomatoes

  .... sevmiyorum.
  Yağmur
  Domates

  ... sevmiyorum
  ya:mur
  domates

- I hate...

  ...-den/dan/ten/tan
  nefret ediyorum.

  ...-den/dan/ten/tan
  nefret ediyorum

  swimming

  Yüzmek

  yewzmek

- Do you like...

  ...-(y)ı/i/u/ü seviyor
  musunuz?

  ...(y)uh/i/u/ew seviyor
  musunuz

  climbing?

  Tırmanmak

  tuhrmanmak

- I like it/them.

  Onu/onları seviyorum.

  onu/onlaruh seviyorum

- I don't like it/
  them.

  Onu/onları
  sevmiyorum.

  onu/onlaruh
  sevmiyorum

✳ feelings and opinions

- I'm very tired.

  Çok yorgunum.

  chok yorgunum

general conversation

33

Are you (very)...		
cold?	Üşüdünüz mü?	ewshewdewnewzmew
hot?	Sıcakladınız mı?	suhjakladuhnuhzmuh
I'm (just)...	(sadece)...	(sadeje)...
tired	Yorgunum.	yorgunum
bored	Sıkıldım.	suhkuhlduhm
I'm a bit annoyed.	Biraz kızgınım.	biraz kuhzguhnuhm
What do you think of...?	...hakkında ne düşünüyorsunuz?	...hakkuhnda ne dewshewnewyorsunuz?
I/We think it's...	Bence/bizce...	benje/bizje...
funny	komik	komik
Did you like it?	Beğendiniz mi?	be:endinizmi
I/We thought it was...	Bence/bizce...	benje/bizje...
beautiful	çok güzeldi	chok gewzeldi
awful	çok kötüydü	chok kötewydew
Don't you like it?	Beğenmiyor musunuz?	be:enmiyor musunuz
Do you like him/her?	Onu beğeniyor musunuz?	onu be:eniyor musunuz
I like him/her.	Onu beğeniyorum.	onu be:eniyorum
What's your favourite...?	En beğendiğiniz... ne?	en be:endi:iniz...ne
My favourite... is...	En beğendiğim....	en be:endi:im....
How do people feel about...	...konusunda ne hissediyorlar?	...konusunda ne hissediyorlar
the government?	Hükümet	hewkewmet
the British?	İngilizler	ingilizler
drugs?	Uyuşturucu	uyushturuju

✳ making arrangements

What are you doing tonight?	Bu gece ne yapıyorsunuz?	*bu geje ne yapuhyorsunuz*
Would you like... a drink? to come with us?	...ister misiniz? İçecek bir şey Bizimle gelmek	*...ister misiniz ichejek bir shey bizimle gelmek*
Yes, please.	Evet, lütfen.	*evet lewtfen*
No, thank you.	Hayır, teşekkür ederim.	*hayuhr teshekkewr ederim*
I'd love to.	Çok isterim.	*chok isterim*
What time shall we meet?	Saat kaçta buluşalım?	*saat kachta bulushaluhm*
Where shall we meet?	Nerede buluşalım?	*nerede bulushaluhm*
See you... later at seven	...görüşürüz. Daha sonra Saat yedide	*...görewshewrewz daha sonra saat yedide*
We're looking forward to it.	Onu dört gözle bekliyoruz.	*onu dört gözle bekliyoruz*
Sorry, we already have plans.	Üzgünüm, planımız var.	*ewzgewnewm, planuhmuhz var*
Please go away.	Lütfen gidin.	*lewtfen gidin*
Leave us alone!	Bizi yalnız bırakın!	*bizi yalnuhz buhrakuhn*
What's your email address?	e-posta/e-mail adresiniz ne?	*e-posta/e-mail adresiniz ne*

My email address is … at … dot com.	e-posta/e-mail adresim …. et … nokta com.	*e-posta/e-mail adresim …. et … nokta com.*

✳ useful expressions
(see **essentials**, page 12)

YOU MAY WANT TO SAY…

Congratulations!	Tebrikler!	*tebrikler*
Happy Birthday!	Doğum gününüz kutlu olsun!	*do:um gewnewnewz kutlu olsun*
Happy Christmas!	Mutlu noeller!	*mutlu noeller*
Happy New Year!	Yeni yılınız kutlu olsun!	*yeni yuhluhnuhz kutlu olsun*
Happy Bayram! (Muslim festival)	Bayramınız kutlu olsun!	*bayramuhnuhz kutlu olsun*
Good luck!	İyi şanslar!	*iyi shanslar*
What a pity!	Yazık!	*yazuhk*
Bless you!	Çok yaşa!	*chok yasha*
Have a good journey!	İyi yolculuklar!	*iyi yoljuluklar*
You are welcome!	Bir şey değil!	*bir shey de:il*
Come on in!/Help yourself!	Buyurun!	*buyurun*

travel&transport

* arriving in the country

Turkish entry regulations vary according to nationality. See the Turkish Ministry of Affairs website (www.mfa.gov.tr) for the latest official information.

YOU MAY SEE...

Bagaj	*bagazh*	**baggage reclaim**
Gümrük	*gewmrewk*	**customs**
Çıkış	*chuhkuhsh*	**exit**
Gümrük beyanı	*gewmrewk beyanuh*	**goods to declare**
Pasaport kontrolü	*pasaport kontrolew*	**passport control**

YOU MAY WANT TO SAY...

- **I am here...**
  on holiday
  on business

  ...buradayım.
  Tatil için
  İş için

  ...buradayuhm
  tatil ichin
  ish ichin

- **It's for my own personal use.**

  Kişisel kullanımım için.

  kishisel kullanuhmuhm ichin

- **I am an EU citizen.**

  AB vatandaşıyım.

  AB vatandashuhyuhm

YOU MAY HEAR...

- Pasaportunuz lütfen

  pasaportunuz lewtfen

  Your passport, please.

Ziyaret amacınız nedir?	*ziya:ret amajuhnuhz nedir*	What is the purpose of your visit?
Burada ne kadar kalacaksınız?	*burada ne kadar kalacaksuhnuhz*	How long are you going to stay here?
Nereye gidiyorsunuz?	*nereye gidiyorsunuz*	Where are you going?
...açın lütfen. Bu çantayı/ bavulu Bagajı	*...açuhn lewtfen bu chantayuh/ bavulu bagazhuh*	Please open... this bag/suitcase. the boot.
Benimle gelin lütfen.	*benimle gelin lewtfen*	Come along with me, please.

* directions

sanat galerisi	*sanat galerisi*	art gallery
kale	*kale*	castle
katedral	*katedral*	cathedral
kilise	*kilise*	church
hisar	*hisar*	fortress
hastane	*hastane*	hospital
pazar yeri	*pazar yeri*	market place
cami	*ja:mi*	mosque
müze	*mewze*	museum
park yapmak yasaktır	*park yapmak yasaktuhr*	no parking
geçiş yok/yasak	*gechish yok/yasak*	no trespassing
saray	*saray*	palace

travel and transport

39

directions

özel mülk	*özel mewlk*	**private property**
meydan	*meydan*	**square**
istasyon	*istasyon*	**station**
cadde/sokak	*jadde/sokak*	**street**

Excuse me, please.	Affedersiniz.	*affedersiniz*
Where is...	...nerede?	*...nerede*
the tourist office?	Turizm Danışma Bürosu	*turizm danuhshma bewrosu*
the station?	İstasyon	*istasyon*
Where are...	...nerede?	*...nerede*
the toilets?	Tuvaletler	*tuvaletler*
How do I get to...	...nasıl giderim?	*...nasuhl giderim?*
the airport?	Havaalanına	*havaalanuhna*
the beach?	Sahile	*sahile*
I'm lost.	Kayboldum.	*kayboldum*
We're lost.	Kaybolduk.	*kaybolduk*
Is this the right way to...?	...için bu yön doğru mu?	*...ichin bu yön do:rumu*
Can you show me on the map, please?	Haritada gösterir misiniz?	*haritada gösterir misiniz*
Is it far?	Uzak mı?	*uzakmuh*

travel and transport

- **Is there...** ...var mı yakınlarda? *...varmuh yakuhnlarda*
  - **a bank near here?** Banka *banka*
  - **a supermarket near here?** Süpermarket *sewpermarket*
  - **an internet café near here?** İnternet café *internet kafe*

- **Where is the nearest...?** En yakın...nerede? *en yakuhn...nerede*

YOU MAY HEAR...

Buradayız.	*buradayuhz*	We are here.
Bu taraf/yön.	*bu taraf/yön*	This way.
Şu taraf/yön.	*shu taraf/yön*	That way.
Dosdoğru.	*dosdo:ru*	Straight on.
...dönün.	*...dönewn*	Turn...
Sağa	*sa:a*	right
Sola	*sola*	left
...kadar devam edin.	*...kadar devam edin*	Go on...
Bu caddenin/ sokağın sonuna	*bu jaddenin/soka: uhn sonuna*	to the end of the street
Trafik ışıklarına	*trafik uhshuhklaruhna*	to the traffic lights
İlk...dönün.	*ilk...dönewn*	Take the first on the...
Sağa	*sağa*	right
Sola	*sola*	left

travel and transport

information and tickets

...önünde	...önewnde	in front of...
...karşısında	...karshuhsuhnda	opposite
...arkasında	...arkasuhnda	behind
...yakınında	...yakuhnuhnda	close to...
...yanında	...yanuhnda	next to...

It's...

Çok yakın/uzak.	chok yakuhn/uzak	It's very near/far away.
Beş dakika ötede/ uzakta.	besh dakika ötede/ uzakta	It's five minutes away.
...numaralı otobüse binmeniz lazım.	...numaraluh otobewse binmeniz la:zuhm	You have to take bus number...

✱ information and tickets
(see **telling the time**, page 18)

(see **telling the time**, page 18)

YOU MAY WANT TO SAY...

What time is the... next train	...saat kaçta? Bir sonraki tren	...saat kachta bir sonraki tren
What time does it arrive in...?	...e/a kaçta varıyor?	...e/a kachta varuhyor
Do I have to change?	Aktarma yapmam lazım mı?	aktarma yapmam la:zuhmmuh
Which platform for...?	...peronu hangisi?	...peronu hangisi
Which bus stop for...?	...otobüs durağı hangisi?	...otobews dura:uh hangisi
Where can I buy... a ticket?	...nereden alabilirim? Bilet	...nereden alabilirim bilet

travel and transport

42

One/Two tickets to ... please.	...e/a bir/iki bilet lütfen.	...e/a bir/iki bilet *lewtfen*
single	gidiş	*gidish*
return	gidiş-dönüş	*gidish dönewsh*
For...	...için	...*ichin*
two adults	İki yetişkin	*iki yetishkin*
two children	İki çocuk	*iki chojuk*
a car	Araba	*araba*
I want to reserve...	...ayırtmak istiyorum.	...*ayuhrtmak istiyorum*
a seat	Bir yer	*bir yer*
two couchettes	İki kuşetli	*iki kushetli*
a cabin	Bir kabin	*bir kabin*
Is there a supplement?	Ek ücret var mı?	*ek ewjret varmuh*
Is there a discount for...	...için indirim var mı?	...*ichin indirim varmuh*
students?	Öğrenciler	*ö:renjiler*
senior citizens?	Yaşlılar	*yashluhlar*

YOU MAY HEAR...

Saat ...-de kalkıyor.	*saat...-de kalkuhyor*	It leaves at...
Saat...-de varıyor.	*saat...-de varuhyor*	It arrives at...
Her on dakikada bir gider.	*her on dakikada bir gider*	They go every ten minutes.
Aktarma yapmanız lazım.	*aktarma yapmanuhz la:zuhm*	You have to change.

Dört numaralı peron.	*dört numaraluh peron*	It's platform/pier number four.
Ne zaman... istiyorsunuz?	*ne zaman... istiyorsunuz*	When do you want to...
gitmek	*gitmek*	travel?
dönmek	*dönmek*	come back?
Gidiş mi, gidiş-dönüş mü?	*gidishmi gidish-dönewshmew*	Single or return?
Sigara içilen mi, sigara içilmeyen mi?	*sigara ichilenmi sigara ichilmeyenmi*	Smoking or non-smoking?
...ek ücret var.	*...ek ewjret var*	There's a supplement of...

∗ trains

● Many trains of the Turkish Railways (TCDD) have sleeping cars, couchettes and restaurant cars. Tickets can be purchased at TCDD offices at railway stations and TCDD-appointed agents.

(see **information and tickets**, page 42)

YOU MAY SEE...		
geliş	*gelish*	arrivals
kuşet	*kushet*	couchettes
gecikme	*gejikme*	delay
gidiş	*gidish*	departure/exit

giriş	*girish*	**entrance**
pazar hariç	*pazar ha:rich*	**except sundays**
danışma	*danuhshma*	**information**
bagaj emanet	*bagazh ema:net*	**left luggage**
kayıp eşya	*kayuhp eshya*	**lost property**
kilitli bagaj dolabı	*kilitli bagazh dolabuh*	**luggage lockers**
ana hat trenleri	*ana hat trenleri*	**main line trains**
peron	*peron*	**platform**
rezervasyonlar	*rezervasyonlar*	**reservations**
yemekli vagon	*yemekli vagon*	**restaurant-car**
yataklı vagon	*yatakluh vagon*	**sleeping-car**
grev	*grev*	**strike**
bilet gişesi	*bilet gishesi*	**ticket office**
tuvalet	*tuvalet*	**toilets**
peronlara gider	*peronlara gider*	**to the platforms**
hatlar	*hatlar*	**tracks**
bekleme salonu	*bekleme salonu*	**waiting room**

YOU MAY WANT TO SAY...

- **I'd like a single ticket to... please.** ...için bir gidiş bilet lütfen. *...ichin bir gidish bilet lewtfen*

- **I'd like a return ticket to... please.** ...için bir gidiş-dönüş bilet lütfen. *...ichin bir gidish-dönewsh bilet lewtfen*

- **Are there lifts to the platform?** Peronlara asansör var mı? *peronlara asansör varmuh*

- **Can I take my bicycle on the train?** Bisikletimi trene alabilir miyim? *bisikletimi trene alabilir miyim*

- **Does this train go to Beşiktaş?** Bu tren Beşiktaş'a gider mi? *bu tren beshiktasha gidermi*

Excuse me, I've reserved...	Affedersiniz,... ayırtmıştım.	*affedersiniz ...ayuhrtmuhshtuhm*
a seat	yer	*yer*
a couchette	bir kuşet	*bir kushet*
Is this seat taken?	Bu yer dolu mu?	*bu yer dolumu*
May I...		
open the window?	Pencereyi açabilir miyim?	*penjereyi achabilir miyim*
smoke?	Sigara içebilir miyim?	*sigara ichebilir miyim*
Where are we?	Neredeyiz?	*neredeyiz*

* buses and coaches

Buses, minibuses and coaches are the most common forms of transportation in Turkey. You should buy bus tickets at bus station ticket offices.

There are frequent day and night coach services between all Turkish cities.

(see **information and tickets**, page 42)

YOU MAY SEE...

Otogar	*otogar*	coach station
Otobüs durağı	*otobews dura:uh*	bus stop
Otobüs	*otobews*	coach
Acil çıkışı	*ajil chuhkuhshuh*	emergency exit

buses and coaches

Giriş	*girish*	**entrance**
Uzun-yol otobüsü	*uzun-yol otobewsew*	**long-distance coach**
Giriş yok	*girish yok*	**no entry**
Çıkış yok	*chuhkuhsh yok*	**no exit**

YOU MAY WANT TO SAY...

Where does the bus to the town centre leave from?	Şehir merkezine otobüs nereden kalkıyor?	*şehir merkezine otobews nereden kalkuhyor*
Does the bus to the airport leave from here?	Havaalanına giden otobüs buradan mı kalkıyor?	*havaalanuhna giden otobews buradanmuh kalkuhyor*
What number is it?	Kaç numara?	*kach numara*
Does this bus go to...	Bu otobüs ... gider mi?	*bu otobews ... gidermi*
the beach?	sahile	*sahile*
the station?	istasyona	*istasyona*
Which stop is it for the...	Hangi durak... durağı?	*hangi durak... dura:uh*
museum?	müze	*mewze*
Can you tell me where to get off, please?	Ineceğim yerde haber verir misiniz?	*ineje:im yerde haber verir misiniz*
The next stop, please.	Bir sonraki durak lütfen.	*bir sonraki durak lewtfen*
Can you open the doors, please?	Kapıları açar mısınız?	*kapuhlaruh açar muhsuhnuhz*

travel and transport

47

YOU MAY HEAR...

Şehir merkezine otobüs buradan kalkıyor.	*shehir merkezine otobews buradan kalkuhyor*	The bus to the town centre leaves from here.
Elli yedi (57) numaralı otobüs istasyona gider.	*elli yedi (57) numaraluh otobews istasyona gider*	The number 57 goes to the station.
Burda mı ineceksiniz?	*burdamuh inejeksiniz*	Are you getting off here?
Affedersiniz, burada ineceğim.	*affedersiniz burada ineje:im.*	Excuse me, I'm getting off here.
Bir sonraki durakta inmeniz lazım.	*bir sonraki durakta inmeniz la:zuhm*	You have to get off at the next stop.
Durağı kaçırdınız.	*dura:uh kachuhrduhnuhz*	You've missed the stop.

* underground

(see **information and tickets**, page 42)

YOU MAY SEE...

Giriş	*girish*	entrance
Çıkış	*chuhkuhsh*	exit
Danışma	*danuhshma*	information
Hat 1	*hat 1*	line 1
Sigara içilmez	*sigara ichilmez*	no smoking
Metro	*metro*	underground

YOU MAY WANT TO SAY...

- **Do you have a map of the underground?** — Metro haritanız var mı? — *metro haritanuhz varmuh*

- **Which line is it for the airport?** — Havaalanına giden hat hangisi? — *havaalanuhna giden hat hangisi*

- **Which stop is it for...?** — Hangisi...durağı? — *hangisi...dura:uh*

- **Is this the right stop for...?** — ...için bu doğru durak mı? — *...ichin bu do:ru durak muh*

- **Does this train go to...?** — Bu tren... -(y) e/a gider mi? — *bu tren... -(y) e/a gidermi*

YOU MAY HEAR...

- İki numaralı hat. — *iki numaraluh hat* — It's line number two.
- Bir sonraki durak. — *bir sonraki durak* — It's the next stop.
- Son duraktı. — *son duraktuh* — It was the last stop.

* boats and ferries

(see **information and tickets**, page 42)

YOU MAY SEE...

vapur	*vapur*	**boats**
kamara	*kamara*	**cabins**

deniz yolculuğu	*deniz yolculu:u*	cruises
feribot	*feribot*	ferry
cankurtaran sandalı	*cankurtaran sandaluh*	lifeboat
cankurtaran yeleği	*cankurtaran yele:i*	life jacket
iskele	*iskele*	pier
liman	*liman*	port
rıhtım	*ruhhtuhm*	quay
nehir gezileri	*nehir gezileri*	river trips

YOU MAY WANT TO SAY...

- **I'd like a return ticket to... please.** | ...için bir gidiş-dönüş bileti lütfen. | *...ichin bir gidish-dönewsh bileti lewtfen*
- **Is there a ferry to... today?** | Bugün...için feribot var mı? | *bugewn...ichin feribot varmuh*
- **Are there any boat trips?** | Hiç vapur gezisi var mı? | *hich vapur gezisi varmuh*
- **How long is the cruise?** | Deniz yolculuğu ne kadar sürüyor? | *deniz yolculu:u ne kadar sürüyor*
- **What is the sea like today?** | Bugün deniz nasıl? | *bugewn deniz nasuhl*

YOU MAY HEAR...

- Vapur... gider. Salı ve Cuma günleri | *Vapur...gider saluh ve juma gewnleri* | **Boats go on... Tuesdays and Fridays**

Deniz...	*deniz...*	The sea is...
sakin	*sakin*	calm
dalgalı	*dalgaluh*	choppy

* air travel
(see **information and tickets**, page 42)

(see **information and tickets**, page 42)

YOU MAY SEE...

Havaalanı	*havaalanuh*	airport
Geliş/Varış	*gelish/varuhsh*	arrivals
Çıkış	*chuhkuhsh*	boarding
Çıkış kapısı	*chuhkuhsh kapuhsuh*	boarding gate
Araba kiralama	*araba kiralama*	car hire
Check-in	*check-in*	check-in
Gümrük	*gewmrewk*	customs
Gecikme	*gejikme*	delay
Çıkış salonu	*chuhkuhsh salonu*	departure lounge
Çıkış	*chuhkuhsh*	departures
Dış hatlar	*duhsh hatlar*	international departures
Bagaj	*bagazh*	luggage reclaim
Güvenlik kontrol	*gewvenlik kontrol*	security check

YOU MAY WANT TO SAY...

- **I want to change/ cancel my ticket.** Biletimi değiştirmek/ iptal etmek istiyorum. *biletimi de:ishtirmek/ iptal etmek istiyorum*

- **What time do I/we have to check in?** Saat kaçta check-in yapmam/yapmamız lazım? *saat kachta check-in yapmam/yapmamuhz la:zuhm*

air travel, taxis

Which gate is it?	Hangi kapı?	*hangi kapuh*
Have you got a wheelchair?	Tekerlekli sandalye var mı?	*tekerlekli sandalye varmuh*
My luggage hasn't arrived.	Bagajım gelmedi.	*bagazhuhm gelmedi*
Is there a bus/ train to the centre of town?	Şehir merkezine otobüs/tren var mı?	*shehir merkezine otobews/tren varmuh*

WORDS TO LISTEN OUT FOR...

çağrı	*cha:ruh*	call
iptal	*iptal*	cancelled
gecikme	*gejikme*	delay
uçuş	*uchush*	flight
kapı	*kapuh*	gate
son çağrı	*son cha:ruh*	last call
dikkat! dikkat!	*dikat dikat*	attention! attention!

✳ taxis

● In some towns shared taxis called DOLMUŞ operate on specific routes. Each passenger pays according to the distance travelled to specific stops.

(see **directions**, page 39)

travel and transport

52

YOU MAY WANT TO SAY...

Is there a taxi rank round here?	Buralarda taksi durağı var mı?	*buralarda taksi dura:uh varmuh*
Can you order me a taxi...	...bana bir taksi çagırır mısınız?	*...bana bir taksi cha:uhrur muhsuhnuhz*
immediately? for tomorrow at nine o'clock?	Hemen Yarın saat dokuz için	*hemen yaruhn saat dokuz ichin*
To this address, please.	Bu adrese lütfen.	*bu adrese lewtfen*
How much will it cost?	Ne kadar tutar?	*ne kadar tutar*
Can you put on the meter?	Taksimetreyi açar mısınız?	*taksimetreyi achar muhsuhnuhz*
I'm in a hurry.	Acelem var.	*ajelem var*
Stop here, please.	Burada durun lütfen.	*burada durun lewtfen*
Can you wait for a few minutes, please?	Biraz bekler misiniz?	*biraz bekler misiniz*
I think there's a mistake.	Sanırım bir hata var.	*sanuhruhm bir hata var*
On the meter it's 20 Lira.	Taksimetrede yirmi lira gösteriyor.	*taksimetrede yirmi lira gösteriyor*
Keep the change.	Üstü kalsın.	*ewstew kalsuhn*
Can you give me a receipt?	Bir makbuz verir misiniz?	*bir makbuz verir misiniz*

hiring cars and bicycles

YOU MAY HEAR... ?

On kilometre uzakta.	*on kilometre uzakta*	It's ten kilometres away.
Yaklaşık 10 lira tutar.	*yaklashuhk on lira tutar*	It'll cost about 10 Lira.
On sekiz Lira.	*on sekiz lira*	That's 18 Lira.
...ek ücret var.	*...ek ewjret var*	There's a supplement...
Her bir bavul için	*her bir bavul ichin*	for each suitcase
Köprü için	*köprew ichin*	for the bridge

* hiring cars and bicycles

YOU MAY WANT TO SAY...

I'd like to hire...	...kiralamak istiyorum.	*...kira:lamak istiyorum*
two bicycles	İki bisiklet	*iki bisiklet*
a small car	Bir küçük araba	*bir kewchewk araba*
an automatic car	Bir otomatik vitesli araba	*bir otomatik vitesli araba*
For one day.	Bir gün için	*bir gewn ichin*
For...	...için	*...ichin*
a week	Bir hafta	*bir hafta*
two weeks	İki hafta	*iki hafta*
Until...	..(y)e/a kadar	*..(y)e/a kadar*
Friday	Cuma	*juma*
the 17th August	On yedi Ağustos	*on yedi a:ustos*

- How much is it...
  per day?
  per week?

  ...kaça?
  Bir günlüğü
  Bir haftalığı

  ...kacha
  bir gewnlew:ew
  bir haftaluh:uh

- Is kilometrage/
  mileage included?

  Kilometraj dahil mi?

  kilometrazh da:hilmi

- Is insurance included?

  Sigorta dahil mi?

  sigorta da:hilmi

- My partner wants
  to drive too.

  Eşim de kullanmak
  istiyor.

  *eshim de kullanmak
  istiyor*

- Is there a deposit?

  Depozito var mı?

  depozito varmuh

- Do you take...
  credit cards?
  travellers'
  cheques?

  ...kabul ediyor musunuz?
  Kredi kartı
  Seyehat çeki

  ...kabul ediyor musunuz
  kredi kartuh
  seyehat cheki

- Can I leave the
  car...
  at the airport?
  in the town centre?

  Arabayı ... bırakabilir
  miyim?
  havaalanında
  şehir merkezinde

  *arabayuh ...
  buhrakabilir miyim*
  havaalanuhnda
  shehir merkezinde

YOU MAY HEAR...

- Ne kadar süre
  için?

  ne kadar sewre ichin?

  For how long?

- ...kim?
  Asıl sürücü
  İkinci sürücü

  ...kim?
  asuhl sewrewjew
  ikinji sewrewjew

  Who's...
  the main driver?
  the second driver?

- Ehliyetiniz lütfen.

  ehliyetiniz lewtfen

  Your driving licence,
  please.

- Sınırsız kilometraj
  var.

  *suhnuhrsuhz
  kilometrazh var*

  There's unlimited
  kilometrage.

travel and transport

55

driving

İlave sigorta istiyor musunuz?	*ilave sigorta istiyor musunuz*	**Do you want extra insurance?**
Yüz Lira depozito var.	*yewz lira depozito var*	**There's a deposit of 100 Lira.**
Arabayı/bisikleti saat altıdan önce getirin lütfen.	*arabayuh/bisikleti saat altuhdan önje getirin lewtfen*	**Please return the car/bicycle before six o'clock.**

* driving
(see also **directions**, page 39)

YOU MAY SEE...

Otopark	*otopark*	car park
Bisiklet yolu	*bisiklet yolu*	bicycle path
Dikkat	*dikkat*	caution
Tehlike	*tehlike*	danger
Tehlikeli viraj	*tehlikeli virazh*	dangerous bend
Yol ayrımı	*yol ayruhmuh*	diversion
Yavaş sürünüz	*yavash sewrewnewz*	drive slowly
Otoyol çıkışı	*otoyol chuhkuhshuh*	end of motorway
Çıkış	*chuhkuhsh*	exit
Garaj	*garazh*	garage
Yol ver	*yol ver*	give way
Sağdan gidiniz	*sa:dan gidiniz*	keep right
Demiryolu geçidi	*demiryolu gechidi*	level crossing
Otoyol	*otoyol*	motorway
Dağ geçidi kapalı	*da: gechidi kapaluh*	mountain pass closed

Giriş yok	*girish yok*	**no entry**
Sollamak yasaktır	*sollamak yasaktuhr*	**no overtaking**
Park yapılmaz	*park yapuhlmaz*	**no parking**
Tek yön	*tek yön*	**one-way street**
Yaya geçidi	*yaya gechidi*	**pedestrian crossing**
Yaya	*yaya*	**pedestrians**
Yol kapalı	*yol kapaluh*	**road closed**
Benzin istasyonu	*benzin istasyonu*	**service/petrol station**
Kaygan zemin	*kaygan zemin*	**slippery surface**
Yavaş	*yavash*	**slow**
Hız limiti	*huhz limiti*	**speed limit**
Dur	*dur*	**stop**
Paralı geçiş	*paraluh gechish*	**toll**
Şehir merkezi	*shehir merkezi*	**town/city centre**
Farlarınızı yakınız	*farlaruhnuhzuh yakuhnuhz*	**use headlights (in tunnel)**

YOU MAY WANT TO SAY...

- **Where is the nearest petrol station?** En yakın benzin istasyonu nerede? *en yakuhn benzin istasyonu nerede*

- **Fill it up with...** ...doldurun. *...doldurun*
  unleaded Kurşunsuz *kurshunsuz*
  diesel Dizel *dizel*

- **50 Lira worth of unleaded, please.** Elli liralık kurşunsuz, lütfen. *elli liraluhk kurshunsuz lewtfen*

- **20 litres of super unleaded, please.** Yirmi litre süper kurşunsuz, lütfen. *yirmi litre sewper kurshunsuz lewtfen*

A can of oil, please.	Bir teneke yağ, lütfen.	*bir teneke ya: lewtfen*
Can you check the tyre pressure, please?	Lastiklerin havasını kontrol eder misiniz?	*lastiklerin havasuhnuh kontrol eder misiniz*
Can you change the tyre, please?	Lastiği değiştirir misiniz?	*lasti:i de:ishtirir misiniz*
Where is the air?	Hava pompası nerede?	*hava pompasuh nerede*

YOU MAY HEAR...

Ne istiyorsunuz?	*ne istiyorsunuz*	What would you like?
Ne kadar istiyorsunuz?	*ne kadar istiyorsunuz*	How much do you want?
Anahtar lütfen.	*anahtar lewtfen*	The key, please.

* mechanical problems

YOU MAY WANT TO SAY...

My car has broken down.	Arabam bozuldu.	*arabam bozuldu*
I've run out of petrol.	Benzinim bitti.	*benzinim bitti*
I have a puncture.	Lastiğim patladı.	*lasti:im patladuh*

travel and transport

Can you telephone a garage?	Bir tamirhaneye telefon eder misiniz?	*bir ta:mirhaneye telefon eder misiniz*
Do you do repairs?	Tamir yapıyor musunuz?	*ta:mir yapuhyor musunuz*
I don't know what's wrong.	Nesi var bilmiyorum.	*nesi var bilmiyorum*
I think it's the... clutch starter motor	Sanırım... debriyaj marş	*sanuhruhm... debriyazh marsh*
The ... doesn't work.	...çalışmıyor.	*...chaluhshmuhyor*
Is it serious?	Önemli mi?	*önemlimi*
Can you repair it today?	Bugün tamir edebilir misiniz?	*bugewn tamir edebilir misiniz*
When will it be ready?	Ne zaman hazır olur?	*ne zaman hazuhr olur*
How much will it cost?	Kaç para tutar?	*kach para tutar*

YOU MAY HEAR...

Nesi var?	*nesi var*	What's wrong with it?
Parça ısmarlamam lazım.	*parcha ısmarlamam la:zuhm*	I'll have to order the parts.
Gelecek Salı günü gelin.	*gelejek saluh gewnew gelin*	Come back next Tuesday.

...hazır olur.	...hazuhr olur	It'll be ready...
Bir saat içinde	bir saat ichinde	in an hour
Pazartesi günü	pazartesi gewnew	on Monday
...tutar.	...tutar	It'll cost...

* car parts

YOU MAY WANT TO SAY...

accelerator	gaz pedalı	gaz pedaluh
alternator	alternatör	alternatör
back tyre	arka lastik	arka lastik
battery	akü	akew
bonnet	kaput	kaput
boot	bagaj	bagazh
brakes	fren	fren
carburettor	karbüratör	karbewratör
distributor	distribütör	distribewtör
engine	motor	motor
exhaust pipe	egsoz borusu	egsoz borusu
fanbelt	vantilator kayışı	vantilator kayuhshuh
front tyre	ön lastik	ön lastik
fuel gauge	benzin göstergesi	benzin göstergesi
gear box	vites kutusu	vites kutusu
gears	vites	vites
headlights	farlar	farlar

ignition	kontak	*kontak*
indicator	sinyal kolu	*sinyal kolu*
radiator	radyatör	*radyatör*
rear lights	arka farlar	*arka farlar*
reversing lights	geri vites lambaları	*geri vites lambaluh*
side lights	sis lambaları	*sis lambaluh*
spare tyre	yedek lastik	*yedek lastik*
spark plugs	buji	*buzhi*
starter motor	marş	*marsh*
steering wheel	direksiyon	*direksiyon*
window	cam	*jam*
windscreen	ön cam	*ön jam*
windscreen wiper	silecek	*silejek*

✳ bicycle parts

YOU MAY WANT TO SAY...

back light	arka lamba	*arka lamba*
chain	zincir	*zinjir*
frame	gövde	*gövde*
front light	ön lamba	*ön lamba*
gears	vites	*vites*
handlebars	gidon	*gidon*
inner tube	iç lastik	*ich lastik*
pump	pompa	*pompa*
saddle	oturak	*oturak*

travel and transport

61

saddle	oturak	*oturak*
spokes	jant teli	*zhant teli*
tyre	lastik	*lastik*
valve	supap	*supap*
wheel	tekerlek	*tekerlek*

accommodation

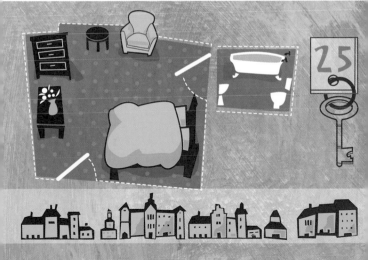

YOU MAY SEE...

Yatak	*yatak*	beds
Kamp yeri	*kamp yeri*	campsite
İçme suyu	*ichme suyu*	drinking water
(Acil) çıkış	*(ajil) chuhkuhsh*	(emergency) exit
Birinci kat/ikinci kat	*birinji kat/ikinji kat*	first floor/second floor
Tam pansiyon	*tam pansiyon*	full board
Garaj	*Garazh*	garage
Zemin kat	*zemin kat*	ground floor
Pansiyon	*pansiyon*	guest House
Spor salonu	*spor salonu*	gym
Yarım pansiyon	*yaruhm pansiyon*	half board
Otel	*otel*	hotel
Çamaşırhane	*chamashuhrhane*	laundry
Asansör	*asansör*	lift
Kamp yapmak yasaktır	*kamp yapmak yasaktuhr*	no camping
Boş oda yok	*bosh oda yok*	no vacancies
Park yeri	*park yeri*	parking
Lütfen zile basınız	*lewtfen zile basuhnuhz*	please ring the bell
Resepsiyon	*resepsiyon*	reception
Restoran/lokanta	*restoran/lokanta*	restaurant
Teras kat	*teras kat*	rooftop terrace
Oda servisi	*oda servisi*	room service
Çöp	*chöp*	rubbish
Sauna	*sauna*	sauna
Duş	*dush*	showers
Tuvalet (Bay)	*tuvalet (bay)*	toilets (m)
Tuvalet (Bayan)	*tuvalet (bayan)*	toilets (f)
Gençlik kampı	*genchlik kampuh*	youth hostel

✱ booking in advance

(see **telephones**, page 138; the **internet**, page 141)

(see **telephones**, page 138; the **internet**, page 141)

YOU MAY WANT TO SAY...

Do you have a ...room?	... odanız var mı?	... odanuhz varmuh
single	Tek kişilik	tek kishilik
double	İki kişilik	iki kishilik
family	Aile için	aile ichin
twin-bedded	İki yataklı	iki yatakluh
Do you have...	...var mı?	...varmuh
rooms?	Boş odanız	bosh odanuhz
space for a tent?	Bir çadır için yeriniz	bir chaduhr ichin yeriniz
I'd like to rent...	...kiralamak istiyorum.	...kira:lamak istiyorum
an apartment	Bir daire	bir daire
a house	Bir ev	bir ev
For...	...için	...ichin
one night	Bir gece	bir geje
two nights	İki gece	iki geje
a week	Bir hafta	bir hafta
from ... to...	...tarihinden...tarihine kadar	...tarihinden...tarihine kadar
only for tonight	Sadece bu gece için	sa:deje bu geje ichin
with...		
bath	Banyolu	banyolu
shower	Duşlu	dushlu
It's a two-person tent.	İki kişilik bir çadır.	iki kishilik bir chaduhr

accommodation

65

booking in advance

How much is it... per night? per week?	...ne kadar? Bir gecesi Bir haftası	...ne kadar bir gejesi bir haftasuh
Is breakfast included?	Kahvaltı dahil mi?	kahvaltuh da:hilmi
Is there... a reduction for children?	...var mı? Çocuklar için indirim	...varmuh Chojuklar ichin indirim
Can I pay by... credit card? travellers' cheques?	...ile ödeyebilir miyim? Kredi kartı Seyehat çeki	...ile ödeyebilir miyim kredi kartuh seyehat cheki
Can I book online?	İnternet üzerinden (online) rezervasyon yapabilir miyim?	internet ewzerinden (online) rezervasyon yapabilir miyim
What's the address?	Adres nedir?	adres nedir
What's your email address?	E-posta/e-mail adresiniz nedir?	e-posta/e-mail adresiniz nedir
Can you recommend anywhere else?	Başka bir yer tavsiye edebilir misiniz?	bashka bir yer tavsiye edebilir misiniz

YOU MAY HEAR...

Ne zaman gelmek istiyorsunuz?	ne zaman gelmek istiyorsunuz	When do you want to come?
Kaç gece için?	kach geje ichin	For how many nights?

accommodation

66

Kaç kişi için?	*kach kishi ichin*	For how many people?
Tek kişilik mi, iki kişilik mi?	*tek kishilikmi iki kishilikmi*	Single or double room?
İki yatak mı istiyorsunuz?	*iki yatakmuh istiyorsunuz*	Do you want a double bed?
Kahvaltı dahil gecesi... Türk Lirası (TL).	*kahvaltuh da:hil gejesi... tewrk lirasuh (tl)*	It's...Turkish Lira per night, including breakfast.
Maalesef, doluyuz.	*maalesef doluyuz*	Unfortunately, we're full.

✳ checking in

YOU MAY WANT TO SAY...

I have a reservation for...	...için rezervasyonum var.	*...ichin rezervasyonum var*
tonight	Bu gece	*bu geje*
two nights	İki gece	*iki geje*
a week	Bir hafta	*bir hafta*
It's in the name of...	...adına.	*...aduhna*

YOU MAY HEAR...

Oda/yer ayırtmış mıydınız?	*oda/yer ayuhrtmuhsh muhyduhnuhz*	Have you reserved a room/space?

accommodation

hotels, B&Bs and hostels

İsminiz/adınız nedir?	*isminiz/aduhnuhz nedir*	**What's your name?**
Pasaportunuz lütfen.	*pasaportunuz lewtfen*	**Can I have your passport, please?**
Kredi kartınızın fotokopisini alabilir miyim?	*kredi kartuhnuhzuhn fotokopisini alabilir miyim*	**Can I take a copy of your credit card?**

REGISTRATION CARD INFORMATION

Adı	*aduh*	**first name**
Soyadı	*soyaduh*	**surname**
Ev adresi	*ev adresi*	**home address**
Uyruğu	*uyru:u*	**nationality**
Mesleği	*mesle:i*	**occupation**
Doğum tarihi	*do:um tarihi*	**date of birth**
Doğum yeri	*do:um yeri*	**place of birth**
Pasaport numarası	*pasaport numarasuh*	**passport number**
Geldiği ülke	*geldi:i ewlke*	**coming from**
Gideceği ülke	*gideje:i ewlke*	**going to**
Tarih	*tarih*	**date**
İmza	*imza:*	**signature**

✳ hotels, B&Bs and hostels

YOU MAY WANT TO SAY...

- **Where can I park?** Arabayı nereye park edebilirim? *arabayuh nereye park edebilirim*

Can I see the room, please?	Odayı görebilir miyim?	*odayuh görebilir miyim*
Do you have...	...var mı?	*...varmuh*
a room with a view?	Manzaralı bir od	*manzaraluh bir oda*
a bigger room?	Daha büyük bir oda	*daha bewyewk bir oda*
a room with air conditioning?	Klimalı oda	*klimaluh oda*
a cot for the baby?	Bebek yatağı	*bebek yata:uhn*
What time is breakfast?	Kahvaltı saat kaçta?	*kahvaltuh saat kachta*
Where is...	...nerede?	*...nerede*
the dining room?	Yemek salonu	*yemek salonu*
the bar?	Bar	*bar*
Is there...	...var mı?	*...varmuh*
24-hour room service?	Yirmi-dört saat oda hizmeti	*yirmi-dört saat oda hizmeti*
an internet connection?	İnternet bağlantısı	*internet ba lantuhsuh*
a business centre?	iş merkezi	*ish merkezi*

YOU MAY HEAR...

Otopark...	*Otopark...*	The car park is...
Otelin altında	*otelin altuhnda*	under the hotel
Yol üzerinde	*yol ewzerinde*	up the road

accommodation

69

camping

Otopark şifreniz (kodunuz) burada.	*otopark shifreniz (kodunuz) burada*	Here's a code for the car park.
Odanızı belki yarın değiştirebiliriz.	*odanuhzuh belki yaruhn de:ishtirebiliriz*	We might be able to change your room tomorrow.
Kahvaltı dahil (değil).	*kahvaltuh da:hil (de:il)*	Breakfast is/isn't included.
Kahvaltı saat.....-den....-e kadar.	*kahvaltuh saat.....-den....-e kadar*	Breakfast is from ... to...
....internet bağlantısı var.	*...internet ba:lantuhsuh var*	There's an internet connection...
İş merkezimizde	*ish merkezimizde*	in the business centre
Odanızda	*odanuhzda*	in your room

* camping
(see **directions**, page 39)

(see **directions**, page 39)

YOU MAY WANT TO SAY...

Is there a campsite round here?	Buralarda bir kamp yeri var mı?	*buralarda bir kamp yeri varmuh*
Can we camp here?	Burada kamp yapabilir miyiz?	*burada kamp yapabilir miyiz*
It's a two/four person tent.	İki/dört kişilik bir çadır.	*iki/dört kishilik bir chaduhr*
Where are... the dustbins?	...nerede? Çöp kutuları	*...nerede chöp kutularuh*

accommodation

- **Do we pay extra for the showers?** — Duş için ek ücret ödüyor muyuz? — *dush ichin ek ewjret ödewyor muyuz*

- **Is this water drinkable?** — Bu su içilebilir mi? — *bu su ichilebilirmi*

- **Where's the electric point?** — Elektrik prizi nerede? — *elektrik prizi nerede*

YOU MAY HEAR...

- En yakın kamp yeri... — *en yakuhn kamp yeri...* — The nearest campsite is...
  - beş kilomete sonra — *besh kilomete sonra* — five kilometres away
  - bir sonraki köyde — *bir sonraki köyde* — in the next village

- Haritanız var mı? — *haritanuhz varmuh* — Have you got a map?

- Burada kamp yapamazsınız. — *burada kamp yapamazsuhnuhz* — You can't camp here.

- Duş ücretsiz. — *dush ewjretsiz* — The showers are free.

- Duş... Türk Lirası (TL). — *dush... tewrk lirasuh (tl)* — It's ... Turkish Lira for a shower.

- Duş almak için jetonunuz olması gerek. — *dush almak ichin zhetonunuz olmasuh gerek* — You need a token to take a shower.

- Elektrik prizi şurada. — *elektrik prizi shurada* — The electric point is over there.

accommodation

71

* requests and queries

- Are there any messages for me?　Bana mesaj var mı?　*bana mesazh varmuh*

- Is there a fax for me?　Bana faks var mı?　*bana faks varmuh*

- Can I...
  - leave this in the safe?　Bunu kasaya koyabilir miyim?　*bunu kasaya koyabilir miyim*
  - put it on my room bill?　Oda hesabıma yazdırabilir miyim?　*oda hesabuhma yazduhrabilir miyim*

- Can you...
  - give me my things from the safe?　Kasadan eşyalarımı verir misiniz?　*kasadan eshyalaruhmuh verir misiniz*
  - order me a taxi?　Bana bir taksi çağırır mısınız?　*bana bir taksi cha uhruhr muhsuhnuhz*
  - come back later, please?　Daha sonra gelir misiniz?　*daha sonra gelir misiniz*

- Do you have...　...var mı?　*...varmuh*
  - a babysitting service?　Bebek bakma hizmeti　*bebek bakma hizmeti*

- I need...　...istiyorum.　*...istiyorum*
  - another pillow　Bir yastık daha　*bir yastuhk daha*
  - an adaptor　Bir adaptör　*bir adaptör*

- I've lost my key.　Anahtarımı kaybettim.　*anahtaruhmuh kaybettim*

accommodation

I've left my key in the room.	Anahtarımı odada unuttum.	*anahtaruhmuh odada unuttum*

YOU MAY HEAR...

Size bir mesaj/faks var.	*size bir mesazh/faks var*	There's a message/fax for you.
Uyandırma servisi ister misiniz?	*uyanduhrma servisi ister misiniz*	Do you want a wake up call?
Saat kaçta?	*saat kachta*	(For) what time?
Ne zaman için bebek bakıcısı istiyorsunuz?	*ne zaman ichin bebek bakuhjuhsuh istiyorsunuz*	When do you want a babysitter for?
Bir dakika lütfen	*bir dakika lewtfen*	Just a moment, please.

✳ problems and complaints

YOU MAY WANT TO SAY...

Excuse me.	Affedersiniz.	*affedersiniz*
The room is...	Oda..	*oda..*
too hot	çok sıcak.	*chok suhjak*
too small	çok küçük.	*chok kewchewk*
too noisy	çok gürültülü.	*chok gewrewltewlew*

accommodation

73

There isn't any...	...yok.	...yok
toilet paper	Tuvalet kağıdı	tuvalet ka:uhduh
hot water	Sıcak su	suhjak su

There aren't any...	...yok.	...yok
towels	Havlu	havlu

I can't...		
open the window	Pencereyi açamıyorum.	penjereyi achamuhyorum
switch on the TV	Televizyonu açamıyorum.	televizyonu achamuhyorum

The bed is uncomfortable.	Yatak rahat değil.	yatak rahat de:il
The bathroom is dirty.	Banyo pis.	banyo pis
The toilet doesn't flush.	Sifon çalışmıyor.	sifon chaluhshmuhyor
The washbasin is blocked.	Lavabo tıkalı.	lavabo tuhkaluh
The light/key doesn't work.	Lamba/anahtar çalışmıyor.	lamba/anahtar chaluhshmuhyor
The microwave/remote control is broken.	Mikrodalga/uzaktan kumanda bozuk.	mikrodalga/uzaktan kumanda bozuk
There's a smell of gas.	Gaz kokusu var.	gaz kokusu var
The washing machine is leaking.	Çamaşır makinası su akıtıyor.	chamashuhr makinasuh su akuhtuhyor
I want to see the manager!	Müdürü görmek istiyorum!	mewdewrew görmek istiyorum

YOU MAY HEAR... 🔊

Bir dakika lütfen.	*bir dakika lewtfen*	Just a moment, please.
Tabii.	*tabii*	Of course.
Hemen başka bir tane getiriyorum.	*hemen bashka bir tane getiriyorum*	I'll bring you another one immediately.
Onu yarın sizin için tamir edeceğim.	*onu yaruhn sizin ichin tamir edeje:im*	I'll fix it for you tomorrow.
Maalesef/özür dilerim bugün mümkün değil.	*maalesef/özewr dilerim bugewn mewmkewn de:il*	I'm sorry, it's not possible today.
O benim sorunum değil.	*o benim sorunum de:il*	That's not my problem.
Biz sorumlu değiliz.	*biz sorumlu de:iliz*	We aren't responsible.

* checking out

YOU MAY WANT TO SAY... 💬

The bill, please.	Hesap lütfen.	*hesap lewtfen*
I'd like to...	...istiyorum.	*...istiyorum*
pay the bill and check out	Hesabı ödeyip çıkış yapmak	*hesa:buh ödeyip chuhkuhsh yapmak*
stay another night	Bir gece daha kalmak	*bir geje daha kalmak*
What time do I have to check out?	Saat kaçta çıkış yapmam gerekiyor?	*saat kachta chuhkuhsh yapmam gerekiyor*

Can I...		
have a late check out?	Geç çıkış yapabilir miyim?	*gech chuhkuhsh yapabilir miyim*
leave my luggage here?	Bagajımı burada bırakabilir miyim?	*bagazhuhmuh burada buhrakabilir miyim*

● **There's a mistake in the bill.** Hesapta bir hata var. *hesapta bir hata var*

● **I/We've had a great time here.** Burada çok güzel vakit geçirdik. *burada chok gewzel vakit gechirdik*

YOU MAY HEAR...

Çıkış saat...-de.	*chuhkuhsh saat...-de.*	Check out is at...
Kaç tane çanta?	*kach tane chanta*	How many bags?
Buraya bırakın.	*buraya buhrakuhn*	Leave them here.
Tekrar bekleriz.	*tekrar bekleriz*	Come again!

✳ self-catering/second homes
(see **problems and complaints**, page 73)

YOU MAY WANT TO SAY...

● I've rented...	..kiraladım.	*...kira:laduhm*
a villa	Bir villa	*bir villa*
an apartment	Bir daire	*bir daire*

accommodation

76

My name is...	İsmim...	*ismim...*
Can you give me the key, please?	Anahtarı verir misiniz?	*anahtaruh verir misiniz*
Where is... the fusebox? the stopcock?	...nerede? Sigorta Vana	*...nerede* *sigorta* *vana*
How does the... work? cooker hot water	..nasıl çalışıyor? Ocak Sıcak su	*....nasuhl chaluhshuhyor* *ojak* *suhjak su*
Is there... air-conditioning? another gas bottle?	...var mı? Klima Başka tüp	*...varmuh* *klima* *bashka tewp*
Are there... any more blankets? any shops round here?	...var mı? Başka battaniye Buralarda dükkanlar	*...varmuh* *bashka battaniye* *buralarda dewkkanlar*
Can I borrow... a corkscrew? a hammer?	...ödünç alabilir miyim? Tirbuşon Çekiç	*...ödewnch alabilir miyim* *tirbushon* *chekich*
We need... a plumber (for an emergency) an electrician	...ihtiyacımız var. (Acilen) Su tesisatçısına... Elektrikçiye	*...ihtiyajuhmuhz var* *(ajilen) su tesisatchuhsuhna...* *elektrikchiye*
How can I contact you?	Sizi nasıl bulabilirim?	*sizi nasuhl bulabilirim*

accommodation

self-catering/second homes

What shall we do with the key when we leave?	Ayrıldığımızda anahtarı ne yapalım?	*ayruhlduh:uhmuhzda anahtaruh ne yapaluhm*

YOU MAY HEAR... ?

Sigorta/vana burada.	*sigorta/vana burada*	The fusebox/stopcock is here.
Böyle çalışıyor.	*böyle chaluhshuhyor*	It works like this.
Bu düğmeye basın.	*bu dew:meye basuhn*	Press this button/switch.
Dolapta yedek battaniye/yastık var.	*dolapta yedek battaniye/yastuhk var*	There are spare blankets/pillows in the cupboard.
Cep telefonu numaram...	*jep telefonu numaram...*	My mobile number is...

food&drink

* food and drink

There are lots of kebab houses (kebapçı) in Turkey. The most common kebabs are şiş kebap (small pieces of lamb grilled on small skewers) and adana kebap (spicy meatballs grilled on a metal skewer). Dürüm is wrap-unleavened pita bread with mainly meat filling which you can buy at most kebab houses.

YOU MAY SEE...

(ucuz) bar	*(ujuz) bar*	(cheap) bar
Alkollü ve alkolsüz içecekler	*alkollew ve alkolsewz ichejekler*	alcoholic and soft drinks
Açık hava bölümü	*achuhk hava bölewmew*	area outdoors with tables
Izgara	*uhzgara*	barbecue/grill
Vestiyer	*vestiyer*	cloakroom
Dondurma salonu	*dondurma salonu*	ice-cream parlour
Kebapçı	*kebapchuh*	kebab house
İçkisiz	*ichkisiz*	no alcohol served
Pastane	*pastane*	patisserie
Piknik alanı	*piknik alanuh*	picnic area
Restoran/lokanta	*restoran/lokanta*	restaurant
Kızarmış hazır tavuk	*kuhzarmuhsh hazuhr tavuk*	roast chicken takeaway
Tabldot	*tabldot*	set menu
Büfe	*bewfe*	snack bar
Hazır yemek	*hazuhr yemek*	take-away food
Çayevi	*chayevi*	teahouse
Teras	*teras*	terrace

Tuvalet	*tuvalet*	toilets
Kıraathane/ kahvehane	*kuhraathane/ kahvehane*	traditional café
Pideci	*pideji*	turkish style pizza house
Kredi kartı geçerlidir	*kredi kartuh gecherlidir*	we accept credit cards

✳ making bookings
(see **time phrases**, page 19)

(see **time phrases**, page 19)

YOU MAY WANT TO SAY...

- I'd like to reserve a table for...
  - two people
  - two adults and three children
  - tomorrow evening at half past eight
  - this evening at nine o'clock

  ...için bir masa ayırtmak istiyorum.
  - İki kişi
  - İki yetişkin ve iki çocuk
  - Yarın akşam saat sekiz buçuk
  - Bu akşam saat dokuz

  ...ichin bir masa ayuhrtmak istiyorum
  - *iki kishi*
  - *iki yetishkin ve iki chojuk*
  - *yaruhn aksham saat sekiz buchuk*
  - *bu aksham saat dokuz*

- My name is...   Adım...   *aduhm...*

- Could you get us a table...
  - earlier?
  - later?

  ...bir masa verebilir misiniz?
  - Daha erken
  - Daha geç

  ...bir masa verebilir misiniz
  - *daha erken*
  - *daha gech*

food and drink

81

YOU MAY HEAR...

Masayı saat kaç için istiyorsunuz?	masayuh saat kach ichin istiyorsunuz	What time would you like the table for?
Kaç kişilik?	kach kishilik	For how many people?
Adınız nedir?	aduhnuhz nedir	What's your name?
Özür dilerim, tamamen doluyuz.	özewr dilerim tamamen doluyuz	I'm sorry, we're fully booked.

* at the restaurant

YOU MAY WANT TO SAY...

I've booked a table.	Bir masa ayırtmıştım.	bir masa ayuhrtmuhshtuhm
A table for four, please?	Dört kişilik bir masa lütfen.	dört kishilik bir masa lewtfen
Outside please, if possible.	Mümkünse, dışarda lütfen.	mewmkewnse duhsharda lewtfen
Have you got a high chair?	Bebek sandalyeniz var mı?	bebek sandalyeniz varmuh
How long's the wait?	Ne kadar bekleriz?	ne kadar bekleriz
Do you take credit cards?	Kredi kartı kabul ediyor musunuz?	kredi kartuh kabul ediyor musunuz

food and drink

82

YOU MAY HEAR... ?

Rezervasyonunuz var mı?	*rezervasyonunuz var muh*	Have you got a reservation?
Sigara içilen mi, sigara içilmeyen mi?	*sigara ichilen mi sigara ichilmeyen mi*	Smoking or non-smoking?
Bir dakika lütfen.	*bir dakika lewtfen*	Just a moment, please.
Beklemek ister misiniz?	*beklemek ister misiniz*	Would you like to wait?
kusura bakmayın... doluyuz kapalıyız	*kusura bakmayuhn... doluyuz kapaluhyuhz*	I'm sorry, we're... full closed
Kredi kartı kabul ediyoruz (etmiyoruz).	*kredi kartuh kabul ediyoruz (etmiyoruz)*	We (don't) accept credit cards.

✳ ordering your food

YOU MAY WANT TO SAY... 💬

Excuse me!	Affedersiniz!	*affedersiniz*
The menu, please.	Menü lütfen.	*menew lewtfen*
Do you have... a children's menu?	...var mı? Çocuk menüsü	... *varmuh* *chojuk menewsew*
vegetarian food? a set menu?	Vejeteryan yemeği Tabldot	*vezheteryan yeme:i* *tabldot*

food and drink

83

● We're ready to order.	Sipariş vermeye hazırız.	*siparish vermeye hazuhruhz*
● Can I have...?	...alabilir miyim?	*...alabilir miyim*
● I'd like... for starters for the main course for dessert	... istiyorum. meze olarak Ana yemek olarak Tatlı olarak	*...istiyorum meze olarak ana yemek olarak tatluh olarak*
● I'd first like...and then...	Önce...., daha sonra ... istiyorum.	*önje...., daha sonra ... istiyorum*
● Does that come with vegetables?	Sebzeyle mi getiriyorsunuz?	*sebzeylemi getiriyorsunuz*
● What's this, please?	Bu nedir?	*bu nedir*
● What are today's specials?	Günün yemeği nedir?	*gewnewn yeme:i nedir*
● What's the local speciality?	Bu bölgenin özel yemeği nedir?	*bu bölgenin özel yeme:i nedir*
● I'd like it rare/ medium/well done, please.	Az/orta/iyi pişmiş istiyorum.	*az/orta/iyi pishmish istiyorum*
● Excuse me, I've changed my mind.	Affedersiniz, fikrimi değiştirdim.	*affedersiniz, fikrimi de:ishtirdim*

food and drink

YOU MAY HEAR... ❓

● Önce bir içecek ister misiniz?	*önje bir ichejek ister misiniz*	**Would you like a drink first?**

Sipariş vermeye hazırmısınız?	*siparish vermeye hazuhr muhsuhnuhz*	**Are you ready to order?**
...ne istersiniz?	*...ne istersiniz*	**What would you like for...**
Meze	*meze*	starters?
Ana/sıcak yemek olarak	*ana/suhjak yemek olarak*	the main course?
Tatlı olarak	*tatluh olarak*	dessert?
Maalesef, o bitti.	*maalesef, o bitti*	**I'm sorry, that's finished.**
Nasıl pişmiş istersiniz?	*nasuhl pishmish istersiniz*	**How would you like it cooked?**
...ister misiniz?	*...ister misiniz*	**Would you like...**
Tatlıyı görmek	*tatluhyuh görmek*	to see the
Menüyü	*menewyew*	dessert menu?
kahve	*kahve*	some coffee?

✳ ordering your drinks

- İçki usually refers to alcoholic beverages, while meşrubat refers to soft drinks.

You can order tea, Turkish coffee and soft drinks almost everywhere in Turkey. The most popular drink is çay (tea), served with sugar in glasses. It is traditionally drunk without milk or lemon.

In summer, ayran is a very popular drink in Turkey. It is a yoghurt-based drink with salt.

YOU MAY WANT TO SAY...

- **Can we see the wine list, please?**
  Şarap listesini görebilir miyiz?
  sharap listesini görebilir miyiz

- **A bottle of this, please.**
  Bundan bir şişe lütfen.
  bundan bir shishe lewtfen

- **What beers do you have?**
  Hangi biralarınız var?
  hangi biralaruhnuhz var

- **Is that a bottle or draught?**
  Şişe mi, fıçı mı?
  shishemi fuhchuhmuh

- **Can I have...**
  ...alabilir miyim?
  ...alabilir miyim
    a gin and tonic?
    Bir cin-tonik
    bir jin-tonik
    a whisky?
    Bir viski
    bir viski

- **A bottle of mineral water, please.**
  Bir şişe maden suyu lütfen
  bir shishe maden suyu lewtfen

- **What soft drinks do you have?**
  Hangi meşrubatlarınız var?
  hangi meshrubatlaruhnuhz var

YOU MAY HEAR...

Ne istersiniz?	*ne istersiniz*	What would you like?
Sürahi ister misiniz?	*sewrahi ister misiniz*	Do you want a carafe?
Buz ve limon?	*buz ve limon*	Ice and lemon?
Maden suyu mu normal su mu?	*maden suyumu normal sumu*	Sparkling or still water?

Büyük şişe mi küçük şişe mi?	*bewyewk shishemi kewchewk shishemi*	A large or small bottle?

✳ bars and cafés

- I'll have..., please
  - a Turkish coffee
  - a white coffee
  - a black coffee
  - a cup of tea
  - a apple/herbal tea

  ...lütfen
  Bir Türk kahvesi
  Bir sütlü kahve
  Bir sütsüz kahve
  Bir fincan çay
  Bir elma/bitki çayı

  ...lewtfen
  bir tewrk kahvesi
  bir sewtlew kahve
  bir sewtsewz kahve
  bir finjan chay
  bir elma/bitki chayuh

- with milk/lemon   sütlü/limonlu   *sewtlew/limonlu*

- A glass of...
  - wine
  - apple juice

  Bir bardak...
  Şarap
  Elma suyu

  bir bardak...
  sharap
  elma suyu

- No ice, thanks.   Hayır, buz istemiyorum.   *hayuhr buz istemiyorum*

- A bottle of water, please.   Bir şişe su, lütfen   *bir shishe su lewtfen*

- A piece of...
  - chocolate cake, please.

  Bir parça...
  cikolatalı kek, lütfen

  bir parcha...
  chikolataluh kek lewtfen

- What kind of...
  - sandwiches do you have?

  Neli
  sandviçleriniz var?

  neli
  sandvichleriniz var

food and drink

87

Is there any...	...var mı?	...varmuh
tomato ketchup?	Ketçap	ketchap
salt and pepper?	Tuz ve biber	tuz ve biber
mayonnaise?	Mayonez	mayonez
Same again, please.	Aynısı lütfen	aynuhsuh lewtfen
How much is that?	Ne kadar?	ne kadar

✱ comments and requests

YOU MAY WANT TO SAY...

That was a delicious meal!	Lezzetli bir yemekti.	lezzetli bir yemekti
Can I/we have more...	Biraz daha...lütfen.	biraz daha...lewtfen
bread, please?	ekmek	ekmek
water, please?	su	su
Can I/we have...	...lütfen?	...lewtfen
another bottle of wine	Bir şişe şarap daha	bir shishe sharap daha
another glass	Bir bardak daha	bir bardak daha
...please?		
I can't eat another thing.	Başka birşey yiyemem.	bashka birshey yiyemem

food and drink

YOU MAY HEAR...

Her şey tamam mı?	*her shey tamammuh*	Is everything all right?
Yemeğinizi beğendiniz mi?	*yeme:inizi be:endiniz mi*	Did you enjoy your meal?

* special requirements

YOU MAY WANT TO SAY...

I'm diabetic.	Şeker hastasıyım.	*sheker hastasuhyuhm*
I'm allergic to...	...alerjim var.	*...alerzhim var*
nuts	kabuklu yemiş (fındık/fıstık/ceviz)	*kabuklu yemish (fuhnduhk/fuhstuhk/jeviz)*
cow's milk	İnek sütü	*inek sewtew*
MSG	MSG	*mesege*
shellfish	Kabuklu deniz ürünleri	*kabuklu deniz ewrewnleri*
I'm vegetarian.	Vejeteryanım.	*vezheteryanuhm*
I don't eat meat or fish.	Et veya balık yemiyorum.	*et veya baluhk yemiyorum*
I'm vegan.	Sadece bitkisel ürünler yiyorum.	*sadeje bitkisel ewrewnler yiyorum*
I don't eat any animal product.	Hayvansal gıdalar yemiyorum.	*hayvansal guhdalar yemiyorum*

food and drink

89

I can't eat...	...yiyemiyorum.	*...yiyemiyorum*
dairy products	Süt ürünleri	*sewt ewrewnleri*
wheat products	Tahıl ürünleri	*tahuhl ewrewnleri*
Do you have ...	...yemeğiniz var mı?	*...yeme:iniz varmuh*
food?		
halal	Helal	*helal*
kosher	Koşer	*koşer*
low sodium	Az tuzlu	*az tuzlu*
low fat	Az yağlı	*az ya:luh*
organic	Organik	*organik*
Do you have	Etsiz yemeğiniz var	*etsiz yeme:iniz*
anything without	mı?	*varmuh*
meat?		
Is that cooked with...	... mi/mı pişirildi?	*... mi/muh pishirildi*
butter?	Tereyağlı	*tereya:luh*
garlic?	Sarımsaklı	*saruhmsakluh*
nuts?	Fındık, fıstık,	*fuhnduhk, fuhstuhk,*
	cevizle	*jevizle*
Does that have ...		
in it?	İçinde...var mı?	*ichinde...varmuh*
nuts	Fındık, fıstık, ceviz	*fuhnduhk*
		fuhstuhk/jeviz

YOU MAY HEAR...

Mutfağa	*mutfa:a bakaja:uhm*	I'll check with the
bakacağım		kitchen.
İçinde...var.	*ichinde...var*	It's all got ... in it
tereyağı	*tereya:uh*	butter
sarmısak	*sarmuhsak*	garlic
fındık/fıstık	*fuhnduhk/fuhstuk/*	nuts
ceviz	*ceviz*	

✳ problems and complaints

This is...	Bu...	bu...
cold	soğuk	so:uk
underdone	az pişmiş	az pishmish
burnt	yanmış	yanmuhsh
I ordered the...	...söyledim/istedim.	...söyledim/istedim
Is our food coming soon?	Yemeğimiz geliyor mu?	yeme:imiz geliyormu

✳ paying the bill

● By law, restaurant prices include VAT (KDV). You may see KDV dahildir (VAT included) on the price list. A service charge is usually included in the price but an extra tip of about 5% is appreciated.

The bill, please.	Hesap, lütfen.	hesap lewtfen
Is service included?	Servis dahil mi?	servis da:hilmi
There's a mistake here.	Bir yanlış var.	bir yanluhsh var
That was fantastic, thank you.	Çok güzeldi, teşekkür ederiz.	chok gewzeldi, teshekkewr ederiz

food and drink

91

Servis dahil değil.	*servis da:hil de:il*	**Service isn't included.**
Maalesef, sadece nakit alıyoruz.	*maalesef sadeje nakit aluhyoruz*	**Sorry, we only accept cash.**

✳ buying food

YOU MAY WANT TO SAY...

● I'd like... please.	...lütfen.	*...lewtfen*
some of those/ that	Biraz şundan/ şunlardan	*biraz shundan/ shunlardan*
a kilo (of ...)	Bir kilo	*bir kilo*
half a kilo (of ...)	Yarım kilo	*yaruhm kilo*
two hundred grammes of that	Şundan iki yüz gram	*shundan iki yewz gram*
a piece of that	Şundan bir parça	*shundan bir parcha*
two slices of that	Şundan iki dilim	*shundan iki dilim*
● How much is...	...ne kadar?	*...ne kadar*
that?	Şu	*shu*
a kilo of cheese?	Bir kilo peynir	*bir kilo peynir*
● What's that, please?	Şu nedir?	*shu nedir*
● Have you got...	...var mı?	*...varmuh*
any bread?	Ekmek	*ekmek*
any more?	Başka	*bashka*
● A bit more/less, please.	Biraz daha fazla/az lütfen.	*biraz daha fazla/az lewtfen*

- **That's enough, thank you.** | Yeterli, teşekkür ederim. | *yeterli teshekkewr ederim*
- **That's all, thank you.** | Hepsi bu kadar, teşekkür ederim. | *hepsi bu kadar, teshekkewr ederim*
- **Can I have a bag, please?** | Bir poşet alabilir miyim? | *bir poshet alabilir miyim*

YOU MAY HEAR...

Yardım edebilir miyim?	*yarduhm edebilir miyim*	**Can I help you?**
Ne kadar istersiniz?	*ne kadar istersiniz*	**How much would you like?**
Kaç tane istersiniz?	*kach ta:ne istersiniz*	**How many would you like?**
Maalesef, bitti/ kalmadı.	*maalesef bitti/ kalmaduh*	**Unfortunately, we've sold out.**
Başka bir şey?	*bashka bir shey*	**Anything else?**

menu reader

GENERAL

Meze	*Meze*	assorted starters
Şarap ve ekmek dahil	*sharap ve ekmek da:hil*	bread and wine included
Kahvaltı	*kahvaltuh*	breakfast
Akşam yemeği	*aksham yeme:i*	dinner
Günün yemeği	*gewnewn yeme:i*	dish of the day
Ev yapımı	*ev yapuhmuh*	home cooking
Öğle yemeği	*ö:le yeme:i*	lunch
Servis dahil (değil)	*servis da:hil (de:il)*	service (not) included
Yemek listesi	*yemek listesi*	set dishes
Tabldot (günün menüsü)	*tabldot (gewnewn menewsew)*	set menu/menu of the day
Ordövr	*ordövr*	starters
Bölgenin özel yemekleri	*bölgenin özel yemekleri*	typical dishes
Zeytinyağlılar	*Zeytinya:luhlar*	vegetables cooked with olive oil
Kredi kartı geçmektedir (geçmemektedir)	*kredi kartuh gechmektedir (gechmemektedir)*	we (don't) accept credit cards

DRINKS

rakı	*rakuh*	arrak, anise brandy
şişe	*shishe*	bottle
brendi	*brendi*	brandy

food and drink

bira	*bira*	**beer**
alkolsüz	*alkolsewz*	**alcohol-free**
şişe	*shishe*	**bottled**
siyah/dark	*siyah/dark*	**dark**
fıçı	*fuhchuh*	**draught**
papatya çayı	*papatya chayuh*	**camomile tea**
şampanya	*shampanya*	**champagne**
çikolata (sıcak/soğuk)	*chikolata (suhjak/so:uk)*	**chocolate (hot/cold)**
şıra	*shuhra*	**cider**
kokteyl	*kokteyl*	**cocktail**
bir bardak fıçı bira	*bir bardak fuhchuh bira*	**a glass of draught beer**
kahve	*kahve*	**coffee**
sütsüz	*sewtsewz*	**black**
kafeinsiz	*kafeinsiz*	**decaffeinated**
buzlu	*buzlu*	**iced**
sütlü	*sewtlew*	**white**
buzlu içecek	*buzlu ichejek*	**crushed iced drink**
fıçı bira	*fuhchuh bira*	**draught beer**
sek	*sek*	**dry**
cin-tonik	*jin-tonik*	**gin and tonic**
bardak	*bardak*	**glass**
kadeh	*kadeh*	**glass for wine**
bitki çayı	*bitki chayuh*	**herbal tea**
buz	*buz*	**ice**
buzlu çay	*buzlu chay*	**iced tea**
sürahi	*sewrahi*	**jug, pitcher**
suyu	*suyu*	**juice**
greyfurt	*greyfurt*	**grapefruit**
limon	*limon*	**lemon**

food and drink

portakal	*portakal*	orange
ananas	*ananas*	pineapple
domates	*domates*	tomato
limonata	*limonata*	lemonade
likör	*likör*	liqueur
dömi-sek	*dömi-sek*	medium dry
süt (sıcak/soğuk)	*sewt (suhjak/so:uk)*	milk (hot/cold)
maden suyu	*maden suyu*	mineral water
(köpüklü/köpüksüz)	*(köpewklew/köpewksewz)*	(fizzy/still)
nane çayı	*nane chayuh*	mint tea
rom	*rom*	rum
zencefilli bira	*zenjefilli bira*	shandy
soda	*soda*	soda
köpüklü	*köpewklew*	sparkling
tatlı	*tatluh*	sweet
sütlü/limonlu çay	*sewtlew/limonlu chay*	tea with milk/lemon
tonik	*tonik*	tonic
Türk kahvesi	*tewrk kahvesi*	Turkish coffee
şekerli	*shekerli*	sweet
sade	*sa:de*	without sugar
bağbozumu şarap	*ba:bozumu sharap*	vintage
votka	*votka*	vodka
şarap	*sharap*	wine
sek	*sek*	dry
ev şarabı	*ev şarabuh*	house wine
yerli	*yerli*	local wine
kırmızı	*kuhrmuhzuh*	red
pembe /roze	*pembe /roze*	rosé
tatlı	*tatluh*	sweet

tatlı	*tatluh*	sweet
beyaz	*beyaz*	white
viski	*viski*	whisky
ayran	*ayran*	yoghurt-based drink

FOOD

badem	*ba:dem*	almonds
ançüez	*anchewez*	anchovies
elma	*elma*	apple
kayısı	*kayuhsuh*	apricot
enginar	*enginar*	artichokes
kuşkonmaz	*kushkonmaz*	asparagus
patlıcan	*patluhjan*	aubergine
avokado	*avokado*	avocado
jambon	*zhambon*	bacon
simit	*simit*	(Turkish) bagel
fırında pişmiş	*fuhruhnda pishmish*	baked
muz	*muz*	banana
fasulye	*fasulye*	beans
dana eti	*dana eti*	beef
pancar	*panjar*	beetroot
ekmek	*ekmek*	bread
somun ekmek	*somun ekmek*	bread roll
bakla	*bakla*	broad beans
tereyağı	*tereya:uh*	butter
lahana	*lahana*	cabbage

food and drink

havuç	*havuch*	carrot
peynir	*peynir*	cheese
tavuk	*tavuk*	chicken
nohut	*nohut*	chickpeas
hindiba	*hindiba:*	chicory
çikolata	*chikolata*	chocolate
istiridye	*istiridye*	clams
et suyu çorbası	*et suyu chorbasuh*	clear soup
hindistan cevizi	*hindistan jevizi*	coconut
soğuklar	*so:uklar*	cold meats
kabak	*kabak*	courgette
yengeç	*yengech*	crab
krema	*krema*	cream
salatalık	*salataluhk*	cucumber
pastırma	*pastuhrma*	cured spiced beef
ördek	*ördek*	duck
yılan balığı	*yuhlan baluh:uh*	eel
yumurta	*yumurta*	eggs
rafadan	*rafadan*	soft-boiled
haşlama/katı	*hashlama/katuh*	hard-boiled
yağda	*ya:da*	scrambled
rezene	*rezene*	fennel
incir	*injir*	fig
bonfile	*bonfile*	fillet steak
balık	*baluhk*	fish
havyar	*havyar*	fish eggs
pide ekmek	*pide ekmek*	flat bread
taze	*taze*	fresh
hamsi	*hamsi*	fresh anchovies

food and drink

kızarmış	*kuhzarmuhsh*	fried
arnavut ciğeri	*arnavut ji:eri*	fried liver cubes
sigara böreği	*sigara böre:i*	fried rolls with cheese filling
sarımsak	*saruhmsak*	garlic
acur turşusu	*ajur turshusu*	gherkin
keçi	*kechi*	goat
üzüm	*ewzewm*	grapes
kefal	*kefal*	grey mullet
ızgara	*uhzgara*	grilled
helva	*helva*	halva, a Turkish sweet made with sesame
jambon	*jambon*	ham
fındık	*fuhnduhk*	hazelnuts
baharat	*baharat*	herbs
bal	*bal*	honey
humus	*humus*	hummus
dondurma	*dondurma*	ice-cream
kebap	*kebap*	kebab
böbrek	*böbrek*	kidneys
kuzu	*kuzu*	lamb
türlü	*tewrlew*	lamb stew with vegetables
limon	*limon*	lemon
mercimek	*merjimek*	lentils
marul	*marul*	lettuce
karaciğer	*karaji:er*	liver
istakoz	*istakoz*	lobster
yerli	*yerli*	local

food and drink

uskumru	*uskumru*	mackerel
terbiye edilmiş	*terbiye edilmish*	marinated
mayonez	*mayonez*	mayonnaise
köfte	*köfte*	meatballs
kavun	*kavun*	melon
karışık kızarmış balık	*karuhshuhk kuhzarmuhsh baluhk*	mixed fried fish
karışık sebze	*karuhshuhk sebze*	mixed vegetables
mantar	*mantar*	mushroom
midye	*midye*	mussels
hardal	*hardal*	mustard
tel şehriye	*tel shehriye*	noodles
ahtapot	*ahtapot*	octopus
zeytin	*zeytin*	olives
omlet	*omlet*	omelette
soğan	*so:an*	onion
çoban salatası	*choban salatasuh*	onion, tomato and cucumber salad
portakal	*portakal*	orange
istiridye	*istiridye*	oysters
maydanoz	*maydanoz*	parsley
hamur işi	*hamur ishi*	pastry dishes
şeftali	*sheftali*	peach
yerfıstığı	*yerfuhstuh:uh*	peanuts
armut	*armut*	pear
bezelye	*bezelye*	peas
biber	*biber*	peppers
kırmızı	*kuhrmuhzuh*	red
yeşil	*yeshil*	green
acı	*ajuh*	hot

salamura	salamura	pickled, marinated
ananas	ananas	pineapple
domuz eti	domuz eti	pork
patates	patates	potatoes
karides	karides	prawns
kuru erik	kuru erik	prune
tavşan	tavshan	rabbit
kuru üzüm	kuru ewzewm	raisins
ahududu	ahududu	raspberry
çiğ/pişmemiş/ham	chi:/pishmemish/ham	raw
kırmızı lahana	kuhrmuhzuh lahana	red cabbage
barbunya balığı	barbunya baluh:uh	red mullet
kaburga	kaburga	ribs
pilav	pilav	rice
fırında kızarmış	fuhruhnda kuhzarmuhsh	roast
salata	salata	salad
tuz	tuz	salt
sandviç	sandvich	sandwich
sardalye balığı	sardalye baluh:uh	sardines
sos	sos	sauce
sosis	sosis	sausage
sote edilmiş	sote edilmish	sautéed
börek	börek	savoury pastry/flan
büyük tarak	bewyewk tarak	scallops
levrek	levrek	sea bass
çipura	chipura	sea bream
deniz mahsulleri	deniz mahsulleri	seafood
karides	karides	shrimps

füme	*fewme*	smoked
dil balığı	*dil baluh:uh*	sole
çorba	*chorba*	soup
baharatlı sos	*baharatluh sos*	spicy sausage
ıspanak	*uhspanak*	spinach
kalamar	*kalamar*	squid
biftek	*biftek*	steak
güveç/kapama	*gewvech/kapama*	stew
çilek	*chilek*	strawberry
dolma	*dolma*	stuffed
tatlı ve ekşi	*tatluh ve ekshi*	sweet and sour
tatlı mısır	*tatluh muhsuhr*	sweetcorn
kılıç balığı	*kuhluhch baluh:uh*	swordfish
kızarmış ekmek	*kuhzarmuhsh ekmek*	toast
işkembe	*ishkembe*	tripe
alabalık	*alabaluhk*	trout
ton balığı	*ton baluh:uh*	tuna
kalkan balığı	*kalkan baluh:uh*	turbot
hindi	*hindi*	turkey
vanilya	*vanilya*	vanilla
dana eti	*dana eti*	veal
geyik eti	*geyik eti*	venison
sirkeli	*sirkeli*	vinaigrette
ceviz	*jeviz*	walnuts
karpuz	*karpuz*	watermelon
yaban domuzu	*yaban domuzu*	wild boar
yoğurt	*yo:urt*	yoghurt
cacık	*jajuhk*	yoghurt with cucumber

food and drink

sightseeing
&activities

✳ at the tourist office

● Most towns and cities have their own Tourism Information Offices – look for the sign Turizm Danışma Bürosu. You can visit the Turkish Ministry of Culture and Tourism website (www.kultur.gov.tr) for city guides, museums, historical places, archaeological sites etc.

YOU MAY SEE...

Kapalı	*kapaluh*	**closed**
Oteller	*oteller*	**hotels**
Broşürler	*broshewrler*	**leaflets**
Haritalar	*haritalar*	**maps**
Açık	*achuhk*	**open**
Biletler	*biletler*	**tickets**

YOU MAY WANT TO SAY...

● **Do you speak English?**	İngilizce biliyor musunuz?	*ingilizje biliyor musunuz*
● **Do you have...**	...var mı?	*...varmuh*
a map of the town?	Şehrin haritası	*shehrin haritasuh*
a list of hotels?	Otellerin listesi	*otellerin listesi*
● **Can you recommend...**	...tavsiye edebilir misiniz?	*...tavsiye edebilir misiniz*
a cheap hotel?	Ucuz bir otel	*ujuz bir otel*

sightseeing and activities

a good campsite?	İyi bir kamp yeri	*iyi bir kamp yeri*
a traditional restaurant?	Geleneksel bir restoran/ lokanta?	*geleneksel bir restoran/lokanta*
● Do you have information...	...bilgi var mı?	*...bilgi varmuh*
in English?	İngilizce	*ingilizje*
● Can you book...	...ayırtabilir misiniz?	*...ayuhrtabilir misiniz*
a hotel room for me?	Benim için bir otel	*benim ichin bir otel*
this day trip for me?	Benim için bu günübirlik geziyi	*benim ichin bu gewnewbirlik geziyi*
● Where is...	...nerede?	*...nerede*
the old part of the town?	Şehrin eski bölümü	*shehrin eski bölewmew*
the art gallery?	Sanat galerisi	*sanat galerisi*
the museum?	...müzesi	*...mewzesi*
● Is there a post office near here?	Buralarda/Civarda postane var mı?	*buralarda/jivarda postane varmuh*
● Can you show me on the map?	Haritada gösterebilir misiniz?	*haritada gösterebilir misiniz*

✳ opening times

● Opening hours vary for historic buildings, archaeological sites, museums and galleries. Most are closed one day during the week and on the first day of the religious festivals. Check with the local tourist office.

(see **telling the time**, page 18)

sightseeing and activities

YOU MAY WANT TO SAY...

What time does the museum open?	Müze saat kaçta açılıyor?	*mewze saat kachta achuhluhyor*
What time does the... close? archaeological site	...saat kaçta kapanıyor? ören yeri	*...saat kachta kapanuhyor ören yeri*
When does the... open?	...ne zaman açılıyor?	*...ne zaman achuhluhyor*
What time does the museum open?	Müze saat kaçta açılıyor?	*mewze saat kachta achuhluhyor*
What time does the... close? archaeological site	...saat kaçta kapanıyor? ören yeri	*...saat kachta kapanuhyor ören yeri*
When does the... open? exhibition	...ne zaman açılıyor? Sergi	*...ne zaman achuhluhyor sergi*
Is it open... on Mondays? at the weekend?	...açık mı? Pazartesi günleri Hafta sonu	*...achuhkmuh pazartesi gewnleri hafta sonu*
Is it open to the public?	Halka açık mı?	*halka achuhkmuh*

YOU MAY HEAR...

....hariç her gün açık.	*....ha:rich her gewn achuhk*	It's open every day except...

....hariç her gün açık.	....ha:rich her gewn achuhk	It's open every day except...
Saat -den...-e kadar açık.	saat -den...-e kadar achuhk	It's open from... to...
...günleri kapalı.	...gewnleri kapaluh	It's closed on...
Tamir nedeniyle kapalı.	tamir nedeniyle kapaluh	It's closed for repairs.

✱ visiting places

YOU MAY SEE...

Tamir nedeniyle kapalı	tamir nedeniyle kapaluh	closed (for restoration)
El sürmeyiniz/ Dokunmayınız.	el sewrmeyiniz/ dokunmayuhnuhz	do not touch
Giriş	girish	entrance
Çıkış	chuhkuhsh	exit
Rehberli turlar	rehberli turlar	guided tours
Giriş yasak	girish yasak	no entry
Flaş kullanmak yasak	flash kullanmak yasak	no flash photography
Açık	achuhk	open
Açılış/ziyaret saatleri	achuhluhsh/ziyaret saatleri	opening hours
Özel	özel	private
Bilet gişesi	bilet gishesi	ticket office
Giriş ücretsizdir	girish ewjretsizdir	entrance free

YOU MAY WANT TO SAY...

How much does it cost?	Ne kadar?	*ne kadar*
One adult, please.	Bir büyük/tam lütfen.	*bir bewyewk/tam lewtfen*
Two adults, please.	İki büyük/tam lütfen.	*iki bewyewk/tam lewtfen*
One adult and two children, please.	Bir büyük/tam, iki çocuk lütfen.	*bir bewyewk/tam, iki chojuk lewtfen*
Is there a discount for...	...için indirim var mı?	*...ichin indirim varmuh*
students?	Öğrenciler	*ö:renjiler*
senior citizens?	Yaşlılar	*yashluhlar*
children?	Çocuklar	*chojuklar*
people with disabilities?	Özürlüler	*özewrlewler*
Is there...	...var mı?	*...varmuh*
wheelchair access?	Tekerlekli sandalye girişi	*tekerlekli sandalye girishi*
an audio tour?	Audio (işitsel) tur	*audio (ishitsel) tur*
a picnic area?	Piknik alanı	*piknik alanuh*
Are there guided tours (in English)?	(İngilizce) rehberli turlar var mı?	*(ingilizje) rehberli turlar varmuh*
Can I take photos?	Fotoğraf çekebilir miyim?	*foto:raf chekebilir miyim*
Who painted that?	Onu kim yapmış?	*onu kim yapmuhsh*
How old is it?	Kaç yaşında/yıllık?	*kach yashuhnda/ yuhlluhk*

YOU MAY HEAR...

Kişi başına ücret...	*kishi bashuhna ewjret...*	It costs... per person.
...için indirim var.	*...ichin indirim var*	There's a discount for...
Öğrenciler	*ö:renjiler*	students
Yaşlılar	*yashluhlar*	senior citizens
Emekliler	*emekliler*	pensioners
Çocuklar	*chojuklar*	children
...yaşın altındaki çocuklar ücretsiz.	*...yashuhn altuhndaki chojuklar ewjretsiz*	Children under ... go free.
Tekerlekli sandalye rampası var.	*tekerlekli sandalye rampasuh var*	There are wheelchair ramps.
Özür dilerim, tekerlekli sandalyeler için uygun değil.	*özewr dilerim tekerlekli sandalyeler ichin uygun de:il*	I'm sorry, it's not suitable for wheelchairs.
Bir tura katılmak ister misiniz?	*bir tura katuhlmak ister misiniz*	Do you want to join a tour?
Ressam/Mimar...	*ressam/mimar...*	The painter/ architect was...
...-ci yüzyılda yapılmış.	*...-ji yewzyuhlda yapuhlmuhsh*	It was built in the ... century.
...yapılmış.	*...yapuhlmuhsh*	It was painted in...
1912 (bin dokuz yüz on iki)'de	*1912 (bin dokuz yewz on iki)'de*	1912
Seksenlerde	*seksenlerde*	the eighties

* going on tours and trips

YOU MAY WANT TO SAY...

I/We'd like to join the tour to...	...turuna katılmak istiyorum/istiyoruz.	...turuna katuhlmak istiyorum/istiyoruz
How long does it last?	Ne kadar sürüyor?	ne kadar sewrewyor
Where does it leave from?	Nereden hareket ediyor?	nereden hareket ediyor
Does the guide speak English?	Rehber İngilizce biliyor mu?	rehber ingilizje biliyormu
How much is it?	Ne kadar?	ne kadar
Is... included?	...dahil mi?	...da:hilmi
lunch	Öğle yemeği	ö:le yeme:i
accommodation	Kalacak yer	kalajak yer
When's the next...	Bir sonraki...ne zaman?	bir sonraki...ne zaman
boat trip?	tekne gezisi	tekne gezisi
day trip?	günübirlik gezi	günübirlik gezi
Can we hire...	...kiralayabilir miyiz?	...kira:layabilir miyiz
an English	Bir rehber	bir rehber
speaking	İngilizce bilen	ingilizje bilen
guide?	bir rehber	bir rehber
I/We'd like to see...	...görmek istiyorum/istiyoruz.	...görmek istiyorum/istiyoruz
I'm with a group.	Bir grupla birlikteyim.	bir grupla birlikteyim
I've lost my group.	Grubumu kaybettim.	grubumu kaybettim

Saat....-de geri dönüyor.	*saat...-de geri dönewyor*	It gets back at...
...-den hareket ediyor.	*...-den hareket ediyor*	It leaves from...
Günlük...ücret istiyor.	*gewnlewk...ewjret istiyor*	He/She charges ... per day.

* tourist glossary

YOU MAY SEE...

Amfitiyatro	*amfitiyatro*	amphitheatre
Sanat galerisi	*sanat galerisi*	art gallery
Kale	*kale*	castle
Sur	*sur*	city wall
İmparator	*imparator*	emperor
Sergi	*sergi*	exhibition
Peri bacası	*peri bajasuh*	fairy chimney
Hisar/kale	*hisar/kale*	fortress
Bahçeler	*bahcheler*	gardens
Kaplıca	*kapluhja*	hot springs
Anıt	*anuht*	monument
Mozaik	*mozaik*	mosaic
Cami	*ja:mi*	mosque
Ressam	*ressam*	painter
Saray	*saray*	palace
Park	*park*	park
Prens	*prens*	prince
Prenses	*prenses*	princess
Kraliçe	*kraliche*	queen
Türbe	*tewrbe*	shrine

sightseeing and activities

111

Hediyelik eşya	*hediyelik eshya*	**souvenirs**
Stadyum	*stadyum*	**stadium**
Meydan	*meydan*	**square**
Sultan/Padişah	*sultan/padishah*	**sultan**
Tapınak	*tapuhnak*	**temple**
Kule	*kule*	**tower**
Şelale	*shela:le*	**waterfall**
Hayvanat bahçesi	*hayvanat bahchesi*	**zoo**

✳ entertainment

● Football is the most popular spectator sport in Turkey. Most professional fixtures take place at weekends. Evening performances at cinemas and theatres and most concerts start around 8.30pm.

YOU MAY SEE...

Bale	*bale*	**ballet**
Sinema	*sinema*	**cinema**
Sirk	*sirk*	**circus**
Vestiyer	*vestiyer*	**cloakroom**
Konser salonu	*konser salonu*	**concert hall**
Balkon	*balkon*	**dress circle**
Maç	*mach*	**match**
Matine	*matine*	**matinée**
Gece kulübü/ gazino	*geje kulewbew/ gazino*	**nightclub**
Opera binası	*opera binasuh*	**opera house**

Orkestra	orkestra	orchestra
Hipodrom	hipodrom	racecourse
Sıra	suhra	row
Bitti	bitti	sold out
Stadyum	stadyum	stadium
Koltuk	koltuk	seat
Ön koltuk	ön koltuk	stalls
Tiyatro	tiyatro	theatre
Üst balkon	ewst balkon	upper circle
Orijinal dilde altyazılı	orijinal dilde altyazuhluh	original language version with subtitles
Sadece 18 yaş üstü için	sadeje 18 yash ewstew ichin	over 18s only
Ara yok	ara yok	there is no interval
Bugünkü gösteri için biletler	bugewnkew gösteri ichin biletler	tickets for today's performance

YOU MAY WANT TO SAY...

- **What is there to do in the evenings here?** Akşamları yapacak ne var? *akshamlaruh yapajak ne var*

- **Is there anything for children?** Çocuklar için bir şey var mı? *chojuklar ichin bir shey varmuh*

- **Is there... round here?** Buralarda/civarda... var mı? *buralarda/jivarda... varmuh*
    a good nightclub iyi bir gece kulübü *iyi bir geje kulewbew*

- **Is there a football match on this weekend?** Bu hafta sonu bir futbol maçı var mı? *bu hafta sonu bir futbol machuh varmuh*

entertainment

What's on	...ne oynuyor?	...ne oynuyor
tonight?	Bu akşam	bu aksham
tomorrow?	Yarın	yaruhn
at the theatre?	Tiyatroda	tiyatroda
at the cinema?	Sinemada	sinemada
What time does the... start?	...saat kaçta başlıyor?	...saat kachta bashluhyor
game	Oyun	oyun
performance	Gösteri	gösteri
What time does it finish?	Saat kaçta bitiyor?	saat kachta bitiyor
How long does it last?	Ne kadar sürüyor?	ne kadar sewrewyor
Do we need to book?	Yer ayırtmamız lazım mı?	yer ayuhrtmamuhz la:zuhmmuh
Where can I get tickets?	Biletleri nereden alabilirim?	biletleri nereden alabilirim
Is it suitable for children?	Çocuklar için uygun mu?	chojuklar ichin uygunmu
Has the film got subtitles?	Film altyazılı mı?	film altyazuhluhmuh
Is it dubbed?	Dublajlı mı?	dublazhluhmuh
Who's...	Kim...	kim...
singing?	şarkı söylüyor?	sharkuh söylewyor
playing? (music)	çalıyor?	chaluhyor
playing? (team sport)	oynuyor?	oynuyor
in that?	var?	var

YOU MAY HEAR...

Saat...-de başlıyor.	*saat...-de bashluhyor*	It starts at...
Saat...-de bitiyor.	*saat...-de bitiyor*	It finishes at...
Dublajlı.	*dublazhluh*	It's dubbed.
İngilizce altyazılı.	*ingilizje altyazuhluh*	It's got English subtitles.
Bileti buradan alabilirsiniz	*biletleri buradan alabilirsiniz*	You can buy tickets here.

✳ booking tickets

YOU MAY WANT TO SAY...

Can you get me tickets for... the football match?	...için bana bilet alabilir misiniz? Futbol maçı	*...ichin bana bilet alabilir misiniz* *futbol machuh*
Are there any seats left for Saturday?	Cumartesi için yer var mı?	*jumartesi ichin yer varmuh*
I'd like to book... a box two seats	...ayırtmak istiyorum. Bir loca İki kişilik yer	*...ayuhrtmak istiyorum* *bir loja* *iki kishilik yer*
Do you have anything cheaper?	Daha ucuz bir şey var mı?	*daha ucuz bir shey varmuh*
Is there wheelchair access?	Tekerlekli sandalye girişi var mı?	*tekerlekli sandalye girishi varmuh*

YOU MAY HEAR...

Kaç tane?	*kach tane*	How many?
Ne zaman için?	*ne zaman ichin*	When for?
Maalesef, o günün/akşamın (biletleri) bitti.	*maalesef o gewnewn/ akshamuh (biletleri) bitti*	Unfortunately, we're sold out that day/night.

* at the show

YOU MAY WANT TO SAY...

Two tickets for tonight's performance, please.	Bu akşamki gösteri için iki bilet lütfen.	*bu akshamki gösteri ichin iki bilet lewtfen*
One adult and two children, please.	Bir büyük/tam, iki çocuk lütfen.	*bir bewyewk/tam iki chojuk lewtfen*
How much is that?	Ne kadar?	*ne kadar*
We'd like to sit... at the front at the back in the middle	...oturmak istiyoruz. Önde Arkada Ortada	*...oturmak istiyoruz* *önde* *arkada* *ortada*
We've reserved seats.	Yer ayırtmıştık.	*yer ayuhrtmuhshtuhk*
My name is...	İsmim/adım...	*ismim/aduhm...*
Is there an interval?	Ara var mı?	*ara varmuh*

- Where's...
  - the balcony?
  - the upper circle?

  ...nerede?
  Balkon
  Üst balkon

  ...nerede
  balkon
  ewst balkon

- Where are the toilets?

  Tuvaletler nerede?

  tuvaletler nerede

- Can you stop talking, please?

  Susar mısınız, lütfen?

  susar muhsuhnuhz lewtfen

YOU MAY HEAR...

- Maalesef bu akşam doluyuz.

  maalesef bu akşam doluyuz

  Sorry, we're full tonight.

- Nerede oturmak istiyorsunuz?

  nerede oturmak istiyorsunuz

  Where do you want to sit?

- Bir program ister misiniz?

  bir program ister misiniz

  Would you like a programme?

✳ sports and activities

YOU MAY SEE...

Plaj	*Plazh*	beach
Teleferik	*teleferik*	cable car
Kano	*kano*	canoe
Kanyon geçişi	*kanyon gechishi*	canyon pass

Teleferik	*teleferik*	chair lift
Tehlike	*tehlike*	danger
Dalış	*daluhsh*	diving
İlkyardım	*illkyarduhm*	first aid
Futbol sahası	*futbol sahasuh*	football pitch
Golf sahası	*golf sahasuh*	golf course
Binicilik	*binijilik*	horse riding
Dağ bisikleti	*da: bisikleti*	mountain bike
Dağcılık	*da:juhluhk*	mountaineering
Balık tutmak yasaktır	*baluhk tutmak yasaktuhr*	no fishing
Denize girmek tehlikeli ve yasaktır	*denize girmek tehlikeli ve yasaktuhr*	it is dangerous and prohibited to go in the sea
Yamaç paraşütü	*yamach parashewtew*	paragliding
Rafting	*rafting*	rafting
Tüplü dalış	*tewplew daluhsh*	scuba diving
Duş	*dush*	shower
Kiralık kayak	*kira:luhk kayak*	ski hire
Lift	*lift*	ski lift
(Kapalı) yüzme havuzu	*(kapaluh) yewzme havuzu*	swimming pool (indoor)
(Açık) yüzme havuzu	*(achuhk) yewzme havuzu*	swimming pool (outdoor)

sightseeing and activities

Tenis kortu	*tenis kortu*	**tennis court**

Where can we...	Nerede...	*nerede...*
play tennis?	tenis oynayabiliriz?	*tenis oynayabiliriz*
play golf?	golf oynayabiliriz?	*golf oynayabiliriz*
I'm...	Ben...	*ben...*
a beginner	yeni başlıyorum.	*yeni bashluhyorum*
quite experienced	çok tecrübeliyim.	*chok tejrewbeliyim*
How much does it cost...	...ne kadar?	*...ne kadar*
per hour?	Bir saati	*bir saati*
per day?	Bir günlüğü	*bir gewnlew:ew*
per week?	Bir haftalığı	*bir haftaluh:uh*
per round?	Bir turu	*bir turu*
per game?	Bir oyunu	*bir oyunu*
Can we hire...	...kiralayabilir miyiz?	*...kira:layabilir miyiz*
clubs?	Golf sopası	*golf sopasuh*
raquets?	Raket	*raket*
Do you give lessons?	Ders veriyor musunuz?	*ders veriyor musunuz*
Can children do it too?	Çocuklar da yapabilir mi?	*chojuklar da yapabilirmi*

sports and activities

YOU MAY HEAR...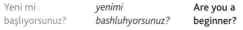

Yeni mi başlıyorsunuz?	*yenimi bashluhyorsunuz?*	Are you a beginner?
Saati... Lira.	*saati... lira*	It costs... per hour.
Geri ödenmek üzere... Lira depozito var.	*geri ödenmek ewzere... lira depozito var*	There's a refundable deposit of...
Maalesef, tamamen doluyuz.	*maalesef tamamen doluyuz*	Unfortunately, we're fully booked.
Daha sonra gelin.	*daha sonra gelin*	Come back later.
Yarın yerimiz var.	*yaruhn yerimiz var*	We've got places tomorrow.
Kaç numara giyiyorsunuz?	*kach numara giyiyorsunuz*	What size are you?
...lazım. Bir fotoğraf Sigorta	*...la:zuhm bir foto:raf sigorta*	You need... a photo insurance
Çok kar yok.	*chok kar yok*	There's not much snow.

* at the beach, river or pool

YOU MAY WANT TO SAY...

- **Can we... swim here?** — Burada yüzebilir miyiz? — *burada yewzebilir miyiz*
- **Is it safe for children?** — Çocuklar için güvenli mi? — *chojuklar ichin gewvenlimi*
- **When is high tide?** — Deniz ne zaman kabarır? — *deniz ne zaman kabaruhr*
- **Is the water clean?** — Su temiz mi? — *su temizmi*
- **Where is the lifeguard?** — Cankurtaran nerede? — *jankurtaran nerede*

YOU MAY HEAR...

- Dikkatli olun, tehlikeli. — *dikkatli olun tehlikeli* — **Be careful, it's dangerous.**
- Dalga çok kuvvetli. — *dalga chok kuvvetli* — **The current is very strong.**
- Çok rüzgarlı. — *chok rewzgarluh* — **It's very windy.**

sightseeing and activities

121

at the beach, river or pool

YOU MAY SEE...

Dalmak yasak.	*dalmak yasak*	**no diving**
Koşmayınız.	*koshmayuhnuhz*	**no running**
Dikkat! Denizanası.	*dikkat denizanasuh*	**danger, jellyfish**

sightseeing and activities

shops&services

✱ shopping

YOU MAY SEE...

(Acil) Çıkış	(ajil) chuhkuhsh	(emergency) exit
Antika	antika	antiques
Fırın	fuhruhn	bakery
Bodrum	bodrum	basement
Kitapçı	kitapchuh	bookshop
Kasap	kasap	butcher's
Pastane	pastane	cake shop
Kasa	kasa	cashier
Eczane	ejzane	chemist's
Çocuk (reyonu)	chojuk (reyonu)	children's
Kapalı	kapaluh	closed
Tasfiye nedeniyle indirim/ucuzluk	tasfiye nedeniyle indirim/ujuzluk	closing down sale
Giyim	giyim	clothing
Bilgisayar	bilgisayar	computers
Şekerci	shekerji	confectioner's
Şarküteri	sharkewteri	delicatessen
Alışveriş mağazası	aluhshverish ma:azasuh	department store
Yapı market	yapuh market	DIY shop
Dokunmayınız	dokunmayuhnuhz	do not touch
Kuru temizlemeci	kuru temizlemeji	dry-cleaners
Elektrikli eşya	elektrikli eshya	electrical goods
Elektronik	elektronik	electronics
Giriş	girish	entry
Moda	moda	fashion
Balıkçı	baluhkchuh	fishmonger's
Giyinme odaları	giyinme odaluh	fitting rooms
Çiçekçi	chichekchi	florist's
Ayakkabı (reyonu)	ayakkabuh (reyonu)	footwear
Mobilyacı	mobilyajuh	furniture shop

Hediye	hediye	gifts
Manav	manav	greengrocer
Bakkal	bakkal	groceries
Kuaför/berber	kuaför/berber	hairdresser's
Nalbur/nalburiye	nalbur/nalburiye	hardware store
Sağlıklı yiyecekler	sa:lıhkluh yiyejekler	health foods
Kuyumcu	kuyumcu	jeweller's
Deri eşya	deri eshya	leather goods
Erkek (reyonu)	erkek (reyonu)	men's
Gazete Bayi	gazete bayi	newsagent's
(Bütün gün) Açık	(bewtewn gewn) achuhk	open (all day)
Gözlükçü	gözlewkchew	optician's
Parfümeri	parfewmeri	perfumery
Eczane	ejzane	pharmacy
Fotoğrafçı	foto:rafchuh	photographer's
Posta kutusu	posta kutusu	post box
Postane	postane	post office
Perakende fiyat	perakende fiyat	retail price
İndirim/ucuzluk	indirim/ujuzluk	sales
Self-servis	self-servis	self-service
Ayakkabıcı	ayakkabuhjuh	shoe shop
Alışveriş merkezi	aluhshverish merkezi	shopping centre
Hediyelik eşya	hediyelik eshya	souvenirs
Özel indirim (fiyatlar)	özel indirim (fiyatlar)	special offers
Spor malzemesi	spor malzemesi	sports goods
Kırtasiyeci	kuhrtasiyeji	stationer's
Süpermarket	sewpermarket	supermarket
Şekerci/tatlıcı	shekerji/tatluhjuh	sweet shop
Tekel bayi/tütüncü	tekel bayi:/tewtewncew	tobacconist's
Oyuncakçı	oyunjakchı	toy shop
Oyuncak	oyunjak	toys
Saatçi	saatchi	watchmaker's
Bayan (reyonu)	bayan (reyonu)	women's

shops and services

YOU MAY WANT TO SAY...

- Where is...
  the post office?
  ...nerede?
  Postane
  ...nerede
  Postane

- Where can I buy...
  suntan lotion?
  a map?
  ... nereden alabilirim?
  Güneş kremi
  Harita
  ...nereden alabilirim
  gewnesh kremi
  harita

- I'd like..., please.
  that one there
  this one here
  two of those
  ...lütfen.
  Şuradaki
  Buradaki
  Şunlardan iki
  tane
  ... lewtfen
  shuradaki
  buradaki
  shunlardan iki
  tane

- Have you got...?
  ...var mı?
  ...varmuh

- How much does it cost?
  O ne kadar?
  o ne kadar

- How much do they cost?
  Onlar ne kadar?
  onlar ne kadar

- Can you write it down, please?
  Yazabilir misiniz lütfen?
  yazabilir misiniz lewtfen

- I'm just looking.
  Sadece bakıyorum.
  sadeje bakuhyorum

- I'll take it.
  Alıyorum.
  aluhyorum

- Can you...
  keep it for me?
  order it for me?
  Benim için ...
  ayırabilir misiniz?
  sipariş edebilir misiniz?
  benim ichin...
  ayuhrabilir misiniz
  siparish edebilir misiniz

- I need to think about it.
  Düşünmem gerek.
  dewshewnmem gerek

YOU MAY HEAR... (?)

Yardım edebilir miyim?	*yarduhm edebilir miyim*	**Can I help you?**
Fiyatı...	*fiyatuh...*	**It costs...**
Maalesef, kalmadı.	*maalesef kalmaduh*	**Unfortunately, we've sold out.**
Sizin için sipariş edebiliriz.	*sizin ichin siparish edebiliriz.*	**We can order it for you.**

✳ paying

YOU MAY WANT TO SAY... 💬

Where do I pay?	Parayı nereye ödüyorum?	*parayuh nereye ödewyorum*
Do you take credit cards?	Kredi kartı alıyor musunuz?	*kuhredi kartuh aluhyor musunuz*
Can you wrap it, please?	Lütfen paket eder misiniz?	*lewtfen paket eder misiniz*
Can I have... please?	...alabilir miyim?	*... alabilir miyim*
a receipt	Fatura/fiş	*fatura/fish*
a bag	Torba	*torba*
my change	Paramın üstünü	*paramuhn ewstewnew*
Sorry, I haven't got any change.	Maalesef, hiç bozuk param yok.	*maalesef hich bozuk param yok*

buying clothes and shoes

YOU MAY HEAR...

Hediye mi?	*hediyemi*	Is it a gift?
Paket edilmesini ister misiniz?	*paket edilmesini ister misiniz*	Do you want it wrapped?
Torba ister misiniz?	*torba ister misiniz*	Do you want a bag?
Lütfen...görebilir miyim?	*lewtfen...görebilir miyim*	Can I see... please?
bir kimlik kartı	*bir kimlik kartuh*	some ID
pasaportunuzu	*pasaportunuzu*	your passport
Bozuk paranız var mı?	*bozuk paranuhz varmuh*	Have you got any change?

* buying clothes and shoes
(see **clothes and shoe sizes**, page 22)

YOU MAY WANT TO SAY...

Have you got...	...var mı?	*...varmuh*
a smaller size?	Daha küçüğü	*daha kewchew:ew*
a larger size?	Daha büyüğü	*daha bewyew:ew*
other colours?	Başka rengi	*bashka rengi*
I'm a size...	...bedenim.	*...bedenim*
I'm looking for...	...arıyorum	*...aruhyorum*
a shirt	Gömlek	*gömlek*
a hat	Şapka	*shapka*

shops and services

128

- **A pair of...** | Bir... | *bir...*
  - **trousers** | pantolon | *pantolon*
  - **sandals** | sandalet | *sandalet*

- **Where are the changing rooms?** | Soyunma odaları nerede? | *soyunma odaluh nerede*

✳ changing rooms

- **Can I try this on, please?** | Bunu deneyebilir miyim? | *bunu deneyebilir miyim*

- **It doesn't fit.** | Uymuyor. | *uymuyor*

- **It's too...** | (O...) | *(o...)*
  - **big** | çok büyük. | *chok bewyewk*
  - **small** | çok küçük | *chok kewchewk*

- **It doesn't suit me.** | Bana yakışmıyor. | *bana yakuhshmuhyor*

Denemek ister misiniz?	*denemek ister misiniz?*	**Would you like to try it/them on?**
Kaç bedensiniz?	*kach bedensiniz?*	**What size are you?**
Size başka bir tane getiriyorum.	*size bashka bir tane getiriyorum.*	**I'll get you another one.**

shops and services

129

exchanges and refunds

Maalesef, o sonuncusu.	*maalesef o sonunjusu.*	Unfortunately, that's the last one.
Size yakıştı.	*size yakuhshtuh.*	It suits/they suit you.

✳ exchanges and refunds

YOU MAY WANT TO SAY... 💬

Excuse me...	Afedersiniz,...	*afedersiniz...*
this is faulty	bu özürlü/defolu	*bu özewrlew/defolu*
this doesn't fit	bu uymuyor	*bu uymuyor*
I'd like...	...istiyorum.	*...istiyorum*
a refund	Para iadesi	*para iadesi*
a new one	Yeni bir tane	*yeni bir tane*
I'd like...	...istiyorum.	*...istiyorum*
to return this	Bunu iade etmek	*bunu iade etmek*
to change this	Bunu değiştirmek	*bunu de:ishtirmek*

YOU MAY HEAR... ❓

...var mı?	*...varmuh*	Have you got...
Faturası	*faturasuh*	the receipt?
Özür dilerim, para iadesi yapmıyoruz.	*özewr dilerim para iadesi yapmuhyoruz*	I am sorry, we don't give refunds.
Değiştirebilirsiniz.	*de:ishtirebilirsiniz*	You can exchange it.

shops and services

130

✳ bargaining

Is this your best price?	Son fiyatınız bu mu?	*son fiyatuhnuhz bumu*
It's too expensive.	Çok pahalı.	*chok pahaluh*
Is there a discount for cash?	Nakit ödemede indirim var mı?	*nakit ödemede indirim varmuh*
I'll give you...	...vereceğim.	*...vereje:im*
That's my final offer.	Bu benim son teklifim.	*bu benim son teklifim*
Take it or leave it.	Son teklifim bu. Ya kabul edin ya da bırakıyorum.	*son teklifim bu. Ya kabul edin ya da buhrakuhyorum*

✳ at the drugstore
(see **at the chemist's**, page 144)

I need...	...lazım.	*...la:zuhm*
aftersun	Güneş sonrası kremi	*gewnesh sonrasuh kremi*
deodorant	Deodorant	*deodorant*
sanitary towels	Hijyenik ped/bez	*hizhyenik ped/bez*
shampoo	Şampuan	*shampuan*
shower gel	Duş jeli	*dush zheli*
tampons	Tampon	*tampon*
toilet paper	Tuvalet kağıdı	*tuvalet ka:uhduh*
toothpaste	Diş macunu	*dish majunu*

I am looking for...	...bakıyorum	...bakuhyorum
a perfume	Parfüm	parfewm
a (pink) nail varnish	(pembe) Oje	(pembe) ozhe

I'd like some...	...istiyorum.	...istiyorum
make-up remover	Makyaj temizleyici	makyazh temizleyiji

* photography

Can you print photos from a memory card?	Hafıza kartından baskı yapabilir misiniz?	hafuhza kartuhndan baskuh yapabilir misiniz
When will it/they be ready?	Ne zaman hazır olur?	ne zaman hazuhr olur
Do you have an express service?	Ekspres baskınız var mı?	ekspres baskuhnuhz varmuh
Does it cost extra?	Ek (ekstra) ücreti var mı?	ek (ekstra) ewjreti varmuh
How much does it cost... per print?	...ne kadar? Baskısı	...ne kadar baskuhsuh
I'd like... an 8MB memory card, please	...istiyorum/lütfen. 8MB hafıza kartı	...istiyorum/lewtfen 8MB hafuhza kartuh

shops and services

132

at the tobacconist

a disposable camera, please	Tek kullanımlık fotoğraf makinesi	*tek kullanuhmluhk foto:raf makinesi*
● My camera is broken.	Fotoğraf makinem/ kameram bozuk.	*foto:raf makinem/ kameram bozuk*
● Do you do repairs?	Tamir işleri yapıyor musunuz?	*tamir ishleri yapuhyor musunuz*

✱ at the tobacconist

YOU MAY WANT TO SAY...

● Can I have a packet of... please?	Bir paket...alabilir miyim lütfen?	*bir paket...alabilir miyim lewtfen*
● Do you sell...	...satıyor musunuz?	*...satuhyor musunuz?*

shops and services

133

matches?	Kibrit	*kibrit*
lighters?	Çakmak	*chakmak*
● Do you sell cigars?	Puro satıyor musunuz?	*puro satuhyor musunuz*
● Do you sell loose tobacco?	Açık tütün satıyor musunuz?	*achuhk tewtewn satuhyor musunuz*

✳ at the off-licence

YOU MAY WANT TO SAY...

● Have you got any...	...var mı?	*...varmuh*
local wine?	Yerli şarap	*yerli sharap*
imported beer?	İthal/yabancı bira	*İthal/yabanjı bira*
● Is this sweet or dry?	Bu sek mi, tatlı mı?	*bu sekmi tatluhmuh*
● I'll take... please.	... lütfen.	*...lewtfen*
a bottle	Bir şişe	*bir shishe*
a pack	Bir paket	*bir paket*

✳ at the post office

● Post offices are open from 8.30am to 5.30pm Monday to Friday, and until 12.30pm on Saturdays. You will usually see the sign PTT outside a post office. Post boxes are yellow and are also marked PTT.

at the post office

A stamp for... please.	...için bir posta pulu lütfen.	...ichin posta pulu lewtfen
Europe	Avrupa	avrupa
America	Amerika	amerika
Australia	Avusturalya	avusturalya
Five stamps, please.	Beş posta pulu lütfen.	besh posta pulu lewtfen
For...	...için	...ichin
postcards	Kartpostal	kartpostal
letters	Mektup	mektup
Can I send this...	...gönderebilir miyim?	...gönderebilir miyim
registered?	Taahhütlü	taahhewtlew
by airmail?	Uçak mektup postası ile	uchak mektup postasuh ile
by Express mail service?	Acele posta servisi (APS) ile	ajele posta servisi (APS) ile
It contains...	İçinde...var.	ichinde...var
a present	hediye	hediye
something valuable	değerli bir şey	de:erli bir shey
something fragile	Kırılacak bir şey	kuhruhlacak bir shey
Can I have a receipt, please?	Makbuz alabilir miyim?	makbuz alabilir miyim
Do you change money here?	Burada para bozuyor musunuz?	burada para bozuyor musunuz

shops and services

135

at the bank

YOU MAY HEAR...

Nereye gidiyor?	*nereye gidiyor*	**Where is it going to?**
Lütfen tartının üzerine koyun.	*lewtfen tartuhnuhn ewzerine koyun*	**Put it on the scales, please.**
İçinde ne var?	*ichinde ne var*	**What's in it?**
Lütfen bu gümrük bildirim formunu doldurun.	*lütfen bu gewmrewk bildirim formunu doldurun*	**Please fill in this customs declaration form.**

* at the bank

● Banks are open from 9am until 5.30pm Mondays to Fridays. Most banks are closed from 12.30 to 1.30pm.

YOU MAY WANT TO SAY...

Excuse me, where's the foreign exchange counter?	Affedersiniz, kambiyo nerede?	*affedersiniz kambiyo nerede*
Is there a cashpoint here?	Burada bankamatik (ATM) var mı?	*burada bankamatik (ATM) varmuh*
The cashpoint has eaten my card.	Kartım bankamatikte kaldı.	*kartuhm bankamatikte kalduh*
I've forgotten my pin number.	Şifremi unuttum.	*shifremi unuttum*
My name is...	Adım...	*aduhm...*

136

changing money

- **I'd like to...** ...istiyorum. ...*istiyorum*
  - **withdraw some money** Para çekmek *para chekmek*
  - **cash this cheque** Bu çeki bozdurmak *bu cheki bozdurmak*

- **Has my money arrived yet?** Param geldi mi? *param geldimi*

YOU MAY HEAR... (?)

Kimlik kartınız lütfen.	*kimlik kartuhnuhz lewtfen*	Your ID, please.
Pasaportunuz lütfen.	*pasaportunuz lewtfen*	Your passport, please.
Adınız (isminiz) nedir?	*aduhnuhzz (isminiz) nedir*	What's your name?
Bakiyeniz ...	*ba:kiyeniz ...*	Your balance is...
Daha fazla para alamazsınız.	*daha fazla para alamazsuhnuhz*	We can't let you have any more money.

✱ changing money

- The Turkish unit of currency is the Turkish Lira (TL). There are 100 Kurus (Kr) to 1 Lira. There are coins of 5 Kurus, 10 Kurus, 25 Kurus, 50 Kurus, and 1 Lira, and banknotes of 1 Lira, 5 Lira, 10 Lira, 20 Lira, 50 Lira, and 100 Lira.

shops and services

137

- I'd like to change..., please.
  these travellers' cheques
  one hundred pounds

  ...bozdurmak istiyorum.
  Bu seyahat çeklerini
  Yüz sterlin

  ...bozdurmak istiyorum
  bu seyehat cheklerini
  yewz sterlin

- Can I get money out on my credit card?

  Kredi kartımdan para çekebilir miyim?

  kredi kartuhmdan para chekebilir miyim

- What's the rate today...
  for the pound?
  for the dollar?
  for the euro?

  ....kur bugün ne kadar?
  Sterlin için
  Dolar için
  Avro için

  ....kur bugewn ne kadar
  sterlin ichin
  dolar ichin
  avro ichin

Ne kadar?	*ne kadar*	How much?
Lütfen burayı imzalayın.	*lewtfen burayuh imza: layuhn*	Sign here, please.
Bir sterlin...lira.	*bir sterlin...lira*	It's ... lira to the pound.

✱ telephones

- Most public telephones are card operated. Payphones are also available in Turkish Telecom Subsidiaries (Türk Telekom Bayi), and in many cafés and newsagents.

Where's the (nearest) phone (box)?	(En yakın) telefon (kulübesi) nerede?	*(En yakuhn) telefon (kulewbesi) nerede*
I'd like to... buy a phone card	...istiyorum. Telefon kartı	*...istiyorum. telefon kartuh*
call England	İngiltere'yi aramak	*ingiltere'yi aramak*
make a reverse charge call	Ödemeli arama yapmak	*ödemeli arama yapmak*
How much does it cost per minute?	Dakikası ne kadar?	*dakikası ne kadar*
What's the country code?	Ülke kodu nedir?	*ewlke kodu nedir*
How do I get an outside line?	Nasıl hat alabilirim?	*nasuhl hat alabilirim*
Hello.	Merhaba.	*merhaba*
It's... speaking.	Ben...	*ben...*
Can I speak to...?	...ile konuşabilir miyim?	*...ile konushabilir miyim*
When will he/she be back?	Ne zaman döner?	*ne zaman döner*
I'll ring back.	Tekrar ararım.	*tekrar araruhm*
Can I leave a message?	Bir mesaj bırakabilir miyim?	*bir mesazh buhrakabilir miyim*
My number is...	Numaram...	*numaram...*
It's a bad line.	Hatlar kötü.	*hatlar kötew*

shops and services

139

mobiles

YOU MAY HEAR...

Kim arıyor?	*kim aruhyor*	Who's calling?
Maalesef, burada değil.	*maalesef burada de:il*	Unfortunately, he's/she's not here.
Bir dakika.	*bir dakika*	Just a moment.
Numaranız nedir?	*numaranuhz nedir*	What's your number?
Meşgul.	*meshgul*	It's engaged.
Cevap yok.	*jevap yok*	There's no answer.
Bekler misiniz?	*bekler misiniz*	Do you want to hold?
Affedersiniz, yanlış numara.	*afedersiniz yanluhsh numara*	Sorry, wrong number.

* mobiles

YOU MAY WANT TO SAY...

Have you got...	...var mı?	*...varmuh*
a charger for this phone?	Bu telefon için şarj cihazı	*bu telefon ichin sharzh jihazuh*
a SIM card for the local network?	Yerel ağt için SIM kart	*yerel a:t ichin SIM kart*
a prepaid card?	Hazır kart	*hazır kart*
Can I hire a mobile?	Cep telefonu kiralayabilir miyim?	*jep telefonu kiralayabilir miyim*

What's the tariff?	Tarife nedir?	*tarife nedir*
Are text messages included?	Yazılı mesajlar dahil mi?	*yazuhluh mesazhlar da:hilmi*

✳ the internet

Is there an internet café near here?	Civarda bir internet café var mı?	*jivarda bir internet kafe varmuh*
I'd like to check my emails.	E-postamı/e-mail kontrol etmek istiyorum.	*e-postamuh/e-mail kontrol etmek istiyorum*
How much is it per minute?	Dakikası ne kadar?	*dakikasuh ne kadar*
It's not connecting.	Bağlanmıyor.	*ba:lanmuhyor*
It's very slow.	Çok yavaş.	*chok yavash*
Can you... print this? scan this?	...basabilir misiniz? ...tarayabilir misiniz?	*...basabilir misiniz ...tarayabilir misiniz*
Can I download this?	Bunu bilgisayarıma indiiebilir miyim?	*bunu bilgisayaruhma indirebilit miyim*
Can I use my memory stick?	Kendi flaş belleğimi kullanabilir miyim?	*kendi flash belle:imi kullanabilir miyim*

faxes

Kullanıcı adı	*kullanuhjuh aduh*	**username**
Şifre	*shifre*	**password**
Burayı tıklayınız	*burayuh tuhklayuhnuhz*	**click here**
Bağlantı	*ba:lantuh*	**link**

✳ faxes

YOU MAY WANT TO SAY...

● **What's your fax number?** — Faks numaranız nedir? — *faks numaranuhz nedir*

● **Can you send this fax for me, please?** — Benim için bu faksı çekebilir misiniz? — *benim ichin bu faksuh chekebilir misiniz*

● **How much is it?** — Ne kadar? — *ne kadar*

health&safety

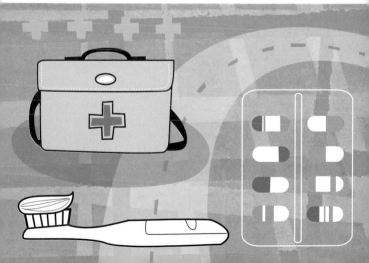

* at the chemist's

● Chemists have the sign Eczane outside. They are generally open from 9am to 7pm. There is always a Nöbetçi Eczane (duty chemist) open all night, and on Sundays and public holidays. The address of the local duty chemist can be found displayed in the window of every chemist's shop. Chemists sell mainly medicines, baby and health products. For toiletries and cosmetics, go to a parfümeri.

(see **shops and services**, page 123)

YOU MAY WANT TO SAY...

● **Have you got something for...** ...için bir şey var mı? ...ichin bir shey varmuh?

sunburn?	Güneş yanığı	gewnesh yanuh:uh
diarrhoea?	İshal/diyare	ishal/diyare
period pains?	Adet ağrısı	a:det a:ruhsuh
headaches?	Başağrısı	basha:ruhsuh
stomach ache?	Mide ağrısı	mide a:ruhsuh
a sore throat?	Boğaz ağrısı	bo:az a:ruhsuh

● **I need some ...** ...lazım. ...la:zuhm.

aspirin	Aspirin	aspirin
condoms	Prezervatif/kondom	prezervatif/kondom
plasters	Yara banti	yara bantuh
travel sickness pills	Araç tutması için hap	arach tutmasuh ichin hap

● **Can you make up this prescription?** Bu reçeteyi hazırlar mısınız? bu recheteyi hazuhrlar muhsuhnuhz

health and safety

144

Bunu daha önce kullandınız mı?	*bunu daha önje kullanduh nuhnuhzmuh*	**Have you taken this before?**
Reçeteniz var mı?	*recheteniz varmuh*	**Have you got a prescription?**

✳ at the doctor's
(see **medical complaints and conditions**, page 147)

YOU MAY WANT TO SAY...

I need a doctor (who speaks English).	(İngilizce bilen) doktor lazım.	*(ingilizje bilen) doktor la:zuhm*
I've run out of my medication.	İlacım bitti.	*ilajuhm bitti*
I'm on medication for...	...için ilaç alıyorum.	*...ichin ilach aluhyorum*
I've had a ... jab.	...aşım var.	*...ashuhm var*
tetanus	Tetanoz	*tetanoz*
typhoid	Tifo	*tifo*
rabies	Kuduz	*kuduz*
He/She has had a ... vaccination.	...aşısı var.	*...ashuhsuh var*
polio	Çocuk felci	*chojuk felji*
measles	Kızamık	*kuhzamuhk*

| Can I have a receipt for my health insurance? | Sağlık sigortam için fatura alabilir miyim? | *sa:luhk sigortam ichin fatura alabilir miyim* |

* describing your symptoms

- To indicate where the pain is you can simply point and say Burası ağrıyor (it hurts here).

(for **parts of the body** see page 150)

(for **parts of the body** see page 150)

YOU MAY WANT TO SAY...

I don't feel well.	İyi hissetmiyorum.	*iyi hissetmiyorum*
It hurts here.	Burası ağrıyor.	*burasuh a:ruhyor*
My... hurts. stomach head	...ağrıyor. Midem Başım	*...a:ruhyor* *midem* *bashuhm*
I've got... a sore throat diarrhoea a bad headache	...var. Boğaz ağrım İshalim/diyarem Kötü başağrım	*...var* *bo:az a:ruhm* *ishalim/diyarem* *kötew basha:ruhm*
I've got swollen glands.	Tükrük bezlerim şişti.	*tewkrewk bezlerim shishti*
I'm dizzy.	Başım dönüyor.	*bashuhm dönewyor*
I feel sick.	Midem bulanıyor.	*midem bulanuhyor*

medical complaints and conditions

- I can't...
  - **breathe properly** — Düzenli nefes alamıyorum — *dewzenli nefes alamuhyorum*
  - **sleep properly** — Düzenli uyuyamıyorum. — *dewzenli uyuyamuhyorum*
- I've been sick. — Kustum. — *kustum*

✱ medical complaints and conditions

- I'm... — ...hastasıyım. — *...hastasuhyuhm*
  - **arthritic** — Eklem romatizması — *eklem romatizmasuh*
  - **asthmatic** — Astım — *astuhm*
  - **diabetic** — Şeker — *sheker*
  - **epileptic** — Epilepsi — *epilepsi*

- I'm... — (Ben...) — *(ben...)*
  - **blind** — körüm — *körewm*
  - **deaf** — sağırım. — *sa:uhruhm.*
  - **pregnant** — hamileyim — *hamileyim*

- I've got... — ...var. — *...var*
  - **high/low blood pressure** — Yüksek/düşük tansiyonum — *yewksek/dewshewk tansiyonum*
  - **a heart condition** — Kalp rahatsızlığım — *kalp rahatsuhzluh:uhm*

- I use a wheelchair. — Tekerlekli sandalye kullanıyorum. — *tekerlekli sandalye kullanuhyorum*

- I have difficulty walking. — Yürüme güçlüğüm var. — *yewrewme gewchlew:ewm var*

- I'm HIV positive. — HIV pozitifim. — *hiv pozitifim*

medical complaints and conditions

I'm allergic to...	...alerjim var.	... *alerzhim var*
antibiotics	Antibiyotik	*antibiyotik*
cortisone	Kortizon	*kortizon*
nuts	Kabuklu yemiş (fındık, fıstık, ceviz)	*kabuklu yemish (fuhnduhk, fuhstuhk, jeviz)*
penicillin	Penisilin	*penisilin*
I have...	...var.	...*var*
hayfever	Alerjik nezlem	*alerzhik nezlem*
angina	Göğüs ağrım	*gö:ews a:ruhm*

YOU MAY HEAR... ❓

Neresi ağrıyor?	*neresi a:ruhyor*	Where does it hurt?
Burası ağrıyor mu?	*burasuh a:ruhyormu*	Does it hurt here?
Ne zamandan beri böyle ağrıyor?	*ne zamandan beri böyle a:ruhyor*	How long have you been feeling like this?
İlaç kullanıyor musunuz?	*ilach kullanuhyor musunuz*	Are you on medication?
Herhangi bir şeye alerjiniz var mı?	*herhangi bir sheye alerjiniz varmuh*	Are you allergic to anything?
Kaç yaşındasınız?	*kach yashuhndasuhnuhz?*	How old are you?
Ağzınızı açın lütfen.	*a:zuhnuhzuh achuhn lewtfen*	Open your mouth, please.
Soyunun lütfen.	*soyunun lewtfen*	Get undressed, please.
Ciddi/önemli bir şey değil.	*jiddi/önemli bir shey de:il*	It's nothing serious.

Enfeksiyonunuz var.	*enfeksiyonunuz var*	You've got an infection.
Enfekte olmuş.	*enfekte olmush*	It's infected.
...tahlili lazım.	*...tahlili la:zuhm*	I need a ... test.
Kan	*kan*	blood
İdrar	*idrar*	urine
Gaita	*gaita*	stool
Röntgen lazım.	*röntgen la:zuhm*	You need an X-ray.
İğne yapmam lazım.	*i:ne yapmam la:zuhm*	I'm going to give you an injection.
Günde üç defa alın (kullanın).	*gewnde ewch defa aluhn (kullanuhn)*	Take this three times a day.
Günde iki defa bir tablet/hap alın.	*gewnde iki defa bir tablet/hap aluhn*	Take one tablet twice a day.
yiyecek/su ile	*yiyejek/su ile*	with food/water
Dinlenmeniz lazım.	*dinlenmeniz la:zuhm*	You must rest.
Alkol almamanız lazım.	*alkol almamanuhz la:zuhm*	You mustn't drink alcohol.
Memleketinize döndüğünüzde doktora gitmeniz lazım.	*memleketinize döndew:ewnewzde doktora gitmeniz la:zuhm*	You should see a doctor when you go home.
Hastaneye gitmeniz lazım.	*hastaneye gitmeniz la:zuhm*	You need to go to hospital.
...burkmuşsunuz.	*...burkmushsunuz*	You've sprained your...
Ayak bileğinizi	*ayak bile:inizi*	ankle
Bileğinizi	*bile:inizi*	wrist

parts of the body

...kırmışsınız.	...kuhrmuhshsuhnuhz	You've broken your...
Kolunuzu	kolunuzu	arm
Kaburganızı	kaburganuhzuh	ribs
...var.	...var	You've got...
Gribiniz	gribiniz	flu
Apandisititiniz	apandisitiniz	appendicitis
Bronşitiniz	bronshitiniz	bronchitis
Bir kırığınız	bir kuhruh:uhnuhz	a fracture
Besin zehirlenmeniz olmuşsunuz.	besin zehirlenmeniz olmushsuni	You've got food poisoning.
Kalp krizi.	kalp krizi	It's a heart attack.
Üç gün içinde tekrar gelmeniz lazım.	ewch gewn ichinde tekrar gelmeniz la:zuhm	You must come back in three days' time.

* parts of the body

YOU MAY WANT TO SAY...

ankle	ayak bileği	ayak bile:i
appendix	apandisit	apandisit
arm	kol	kol
artery	damar	damar
back	sırt	suhrt
bladder	mesane	mesa:ne
blood	kan	kan
bone	kemik	kemik
bottom	alt	alt
bowels	bağırsak	ba:uhrsak
breast	meme	meme

English	Turkish	Pronunciation
chest	göğüs	gö:ews
collar bone	köprücük kemiği	köprewjewk kemi:i
ear	kulak	kulak
elbow	dirsek	dirsek
eye	göz	göz
face	yüz	yewz
finger	parmak	parmak
foot	ayak	ayak
genitals	cinsel organlar	jinsel organlar
gland	bez	bez
hand	el	el
head	baş	bash
heart	kalp	kalp
heel	topuk	topuk
hip	kalça	kalcha
jaw	çene	chene
joint	eklem	eklem
kidney	böbrek	böbrek
knee	diz	diz
leg	bacak	bajak
ligament	lif	lif
liver	karaciğer	karaji:er
lung	akciğer	akji:er
mouth	ağız	a:uhz
muscle	kas	kas
neck	boyun	boyun
nerve	sinir	sinir
nose	burun	burun
penis	penis	penis
rib	kaburga	kaburga
shoulder	omuz	omuz
skin	deri	deri
spine	belkemiği	belkemi:i

at the dentist's

stomach	mide	*mide*
tendon	tendon	*tendon*
testicle	testis	*testis*
thigh	kalça	*kalcha*
throat	gırtlak	*guhrtlak*
thumb	başparmak	*bashparmak*
toe	ayak parmağı	*ayak parma:uh*
tongue	dil	*dil*
tonsils	bademcik	*bademjik*
tooth	diş	*dish*
vagina	vajina	*vazhina*
vein	damar	*damar*
wrist	bilek	*bilek*

✳ at the dentist's

YOU MAY WANT TO SAY...

● I need a dentist (who speaks English).	(İngilizce bilen) Bir dişçi lazım.	*(ingilizje bilen) bir dishchi la:zuhm*
● I've got toothache.	Dişim ağrıyor.	*dishim a:ruhyor*
● It (really) hurts.	(gerçekten çok) ağrıyor.	*(gerchekten chok) a:ruhyor*
● It's my wisdom tooth.	Yirmi yaş dişim.	*yirmi yash dishim*
● I've lost ... a filling a crown/cap	...düştü. Dolgum Kronum/kaplamam	*...dewshtew dolgum kronum/kaplamam*

● I've broken my tooth.	Dişim kırıldı.	*dishim kuhruhlduh*
● Can you fix it temporarily?	Geçici olarak takabilir misiniz?	*gechiji olarak takabilir misiniz*

YOU MAY HEAR...

● Ağzınızı açın.	*A:zuhnuhzuh achuhn*	Open wide.
● Çenenizi birleştirin.	*chenenizi birleshtirin*	Close your jaws together.
● Bir film (röntgen) lazım.	*bir röntgen la:zuhm*	You need an x-ray.
● Hamile misiniz?	*hamile misiniz*	Are you pregnant?
● Bir dolgu lazım.	*bir dolgu la:zuhm*	You need a filling.
● Dişi çekmem lazım.	*dishi chekmem la:zuhm*	I'll have to take it out.
● Size... yapacağım.	*size...yapaja:uhm*	I'm going to give you...
Bir iğne	*bir i:ne*	an injection
Geçici bir dolgu	*gechiji bir dolgu*	a temporary filling
Geçici bir kaplama	*gechiji bir kaplama*	a temporary crown

✳ emergencies

● For an ambulance call 112, for the police call 155, and for the fire brigade call 110. For the police force section responsible for traffic matters call 154. A military force called jandarma is responsible for law and order in rural areas call 156.

health and safety

153

YOU MAY SEE...

Acil servis	*ajil servis*	Accident and Emergency
sağlık Ocağı	*sa:luhk oja:uh*	basic medical care centre
poliklinik	*poliklinik*	clinic
ilk yardım	*ilk yarduhm*	first aid
haricen kullanılır	*harijen kullanuhluhr*	for external use only
hastane	*hastane*	hospital
kullanım şekli	*kullanuhm shekli*	instructions for use
zehir	*zehir*	poison
özel klinik	*özel klinik*	private clinic
kullanmadan önce çalkalayınız	*kullanmadan önje chalkalayuhnuhz*	shake before use
muayene saatleri	*muayene saatleri*	surgery times

YOU MAY WANT TO SAY...

- **Call...** ...çağırın. *...cha:uhruhn*
  - **a doctor** Bir doktor *bir doktor*
  - **an ambulance** Bir ambulans *bir ambulans*
  - **the fire brigade** İtfaiye *itfa:iye*
  - **the police** Polis *polis*

- **Immediately!** Hemen! *hemen*

- **Help!** İmdat! *imdat*

- **Please help me/ us.** Lütfen bana/bize yardım edin. *lewtfen bana/bize yarduhm edin*

There's a fire!	Yangın var!	*yanguhn var*
There's been an accident.	Bir kaza oldu.	*bir kaza oldu*
I have to use the phone.	Telefonu kullanmam lazım.	*telefonu kullanmam la:zuhm*
I'm lost.	Kayboldum.	*kayboldum*
I've lost my car keys.	Arabamın anahtarlarını kaybettim.	*arabamuhn anahtarlaruhnuh kaybettim*
I've lost my... son/daughter	...kaybettim. Oğlumu/kızımı	*...kaybettim o:lumu/kuhzuhmuh*
Stop!	Dur!	*dur*

* police

YOU MAY WANT TO SAY...

Sorry, I didn't know it was against the law.	Özür dilerim, yasaya aykırı olduğunu farketmedim/ bilmiyordum.	*özewr dilerim yasaya aykuhruh oldu:unu bilmiyordum*
Here are my documents.	Buyurun, belgelerim.	*buyurun belgelerim*
I haven't got my passport on me.	Pasaportum yanımda değil.	*pasaportum yanuhmda de:il*
I don't understand.	Anlamıyorum.	*anlamuhyorum*

police, reporting crime

- I'm innocent. | Suçsuzum. | *suchsuzum*

- I want a lawyer (who speaks English). | (İngilizce bilen) Bir avukat istiyorum. | *(ingilizje bilen) bir avukat istiyorum*

- I want to contact my... | ...ile konuşmak istiyorum. | *...ile konushmak istiyorum*
  - embassy | Elçiliğimiz | *elchili:imiz*
  - consulate | Konsolosluğumuz | *konsoloslu:umuz*

Ceza ödemeniz lazım.	*Jeza ödemeniz la:zuhm*	You'll have to pay a fine.
Belgeleriniz lütfen.	*belgeleriniz lewtfen*	Your documents, please.
Kimliğinizi belirten herhangi bir belgeniz var mı?	*kimli:inizi belirten herhangi bir belgeniz varmuh?*	Have you got any proof of your identity?
Benimle gelin.	*benimle gelin*	Come with me.
Tutuklusunuz.	*tutuklusunuz*	You're under arrest.

* reporting crime

YOU MAY WANT TO SAY...

- I want to report a theft. | Bir hırsızlık olayı bildirmek istiyorum. | *bir huhrsuhzluhk olayuh bildirmek istiyorum*

- **My... has been stolen.**
  - purse/wallet
  - passport

  ...çalındı.
  - Cüzdanım
  - Pasaportum

  ...chaluhnduh
  - jewzdanuhm
  - pasaportum

- **Our car has been broken into.**

  Arabamıza hırsız girdi.

  arabamuhza huhrsuhz girdi

- **Our car has been stolen.**

  Arabamız çalındı.

  arabamuhz chaluhnduh

- **I've lost my...**
  - credit cards
  - luggage

  ...kaybettim.
  - Kredi kartlarımı
  - Bagajımı

  ...kaybettim
  - kredi kartlaruhmuh
  - bagazhuhmuh

- **I've been...**
  - mugged
  - attacked

  - Soyuldum.
  - Saldırıya uğradım.

  - soyuldum
  - salduhruhya u:raduhm

YOU MAY HEAR...

Ne zaman oldu?	ne zaman oldu	When did it happen?
Nerede?	nerede	Where?
Dış görünüşü nasıldı?	duhsh görewnewshew nasuhlduh	What did he/she look like?
Dış görünüşleri nasıldı?	duhsh görewnewshleri nasuhlduh	What did they look like?

health and safety

YOU MAY WANT TO SAY...

- It happened...   ...oldu.   ...oldu
  five minutes ago   Beş dakika önce   besh dakika önje
  last night   Dün gece   dewn geje

- He/She had...   ...vardı.   ...varduh
  blonde hair   Sarı saçı   saruh sachuh
  a knife   Bir bıçağı   bir buhcha:uh

- He/She was...
  tall   Uzun boyluydu.   uzun boyluydu
  young   Gençti.   genchti
  short   Kısa boyluydu.   kuhsa boyluydu

- He/She was   ...giyiyordu.   ...giyiyordu
  wearing...
  jeans   Kot pantolon   kot pantolon
  a red shirt   Kırmızı bir gömlek   kuhrmuhzuh bir
                                                  gömlek

basic grammar

✱ how Turkish works

Turkish uses endings to express things that in English are expressed using a different word or several separate words. For example, the ending -lik changes an adjective into a noun:

iyi *(iyi)* good   iyilik *(iyilik)* goodness

There are endings for prepositions like 'with' and 'without':

süt *(sewt)* milk   sütlü *(sewtlew)*   sütsüz *(sewtsewz)*
                      with milk   without milk

When suffixes are added, a single word can become an entire sentence, e.g. sinemadayım *(sinemadayuhm)* means 'I am at the cinema': sinema '(the) cinema' – da 'at' – yım 'I am'.

✱ vowel harmony

The building up of words using different endings is governed by a feature of Turkish called 'vowel harmony'. This means that the vowels used in the various endings change in order to rhyme or harmonise with the last vowel of the basic word.

Turkish has eight vowels, divided into 'front' vowels: e, i, ö, ü, and 'back' vowels: a, ı, o, u. If the last vowel of the basic word is a front vowel, then the endings added to it will also contain front vowels, e.g. otel *(otel)* hotel, oteller *(oteller)* hotels. Similarly, if the last vowel is a back vowel, then the endings will also contain back vowels, e.g. oda *(oda)* room, odalar *(odalar)* rooms.

Some endings can have two basic forms. For example, to make a word plural you add -ler *(ler)* to front vowels, and -lar *(lar)* to back vowels. Some endings can have four basic forms, e.g. the ending for 'with' can be -li *(li)*, -lü *(lew)*, -lı *(luh)* or -lu *(lu)*.

You can work out which ending to use by looking at the last letter of the basic word.

	LAST VOWEL OF BASIC WORD				VOWEL USED IN ENDING
endings with two basic forms	e	i	ö	ü	e
	a	ı	o	u	a
endings with four basic forms	e	i			i
	ö	ü			ü
	a	ı			ı
	o	u			u

✷ nouns

The plural is formed by adding -ler *(ler)* or -lar *(lar)* to the end of the noun, according to the vowel harmony rule, e.g. müze *(mewze)* museum, müzeler *(mewzeler)* museums.

If there is a number before the noun, then the noun keeps the singular form, e.g. bilet *(bilet)* ticket, iki bilet *(iki bilet)* two tickets, biletler *(biletler)* tickets.

✷ cases

Turkish case endings take different forms, according to vowel harmony. In some cases, if the basic word ends in a vowel, an extra consonant is added between the word and the ending. In this book, different forms of the word endings are given, where necessary, within the stem of expressions, with the extra consonant in brackets.

CASE	OTEL	ODA
nominative (subject)	otel *(otel)* **hotel**	oda *(oda)* **room**
accusative (object) -i , -ü , -ı, -u *(i, ew, uh, u)*	oteli *(oteli)* **the hotel**	odayı *(odayuh)* **the room**
genitive/possessive (of)	otelin *(otelin)* **of the hotel**	odanın *(odanuhn)* **of the room**
dative (to) -(y)e, -(y)a *([y]e, [y]a)*	otele *(otele)* **to the hotel**	odaya *(odaya)* **to the room**
locative (at, in, on) -de, -da, -te, -ta *(de, da, te, ta)*	otelde *(otelde)* **at/in the hotel**	odada *(odada)* **in the room**
ablative (from) -den, -dan, -ten, -tan *(den, dan, ten, tan)*	otelden *(otelden)* **from the hotel**	odadan *(odadan)* **from the room**

If the basic word ends in ç, f, h, k, p, s, ş, or t you add -te or -ta for the locative, and -ten or -tan for the ablative endings:
otobüs *(otobews)* bus otobüste *(otobewste)* on the bus
sokak *(sokak)* street sokaktan *(sokaktan)* from the street

In written Turkish, when an ending is added to a proper noun (a name or place) there is an apostrophe before the ending:
Ali'yi *(aliyi)* Ali   İstanbul'da *(istanbulda)*
(as in 'I saw Ali')   in Istanbul

✳ common noun endings

'by', 'using', 'with': -le, -la
Add y if the basic word ends in a vowel:

tren *(tren)* train	trenle *(trenle)* by train
su *(su)* water	suyla *(suyla)* with water

'with', 'containing': -li, -lü, -lı, -lu

şeker *(sheker)* sugar	şekerli *(shekerli)* with sugar
süt *(sewt)* milk	sütlü *(sewtlew)* with milk

'without': -siz, -süz, -sız, -suz

şeker *(sheker)* sugar	şekersiz *(shekersiz)* without sugar
süt *(sewt)* milk	sütsüz *(sewtsewz)* without milk

There is no definite article 'the' in Turkish. The indefinite article 'a' or 'an' is the same as the word for 'one' bir *(bir)*. For example, bir bilet *(bir bilet)* can mean 'a ticket' or 'one ticket'.

✳ pronouns

SUBJECT	OBJECT	POSSESSIVE
ben *(ben)* **I**	beni *(beni)* **me**	benim *(benim)* **mine**
sen *(sen)* **you** (informal)	seni *(seni)* **you** (informal)	senin *(senin)* **yours**
o *(o)* **he/she/it**	onu *(onu)* **him/her/it**	onun *(onun)* **his/hers/its**
biz *(biz)* **we**	bizi *(bizi)* **us**	bizim *(bizim)* **ours**
siz *(siz)* **you** (formal/plural)	sizi *(sizi)* **you** (formal/plural)	sizin *(sizin)* **yours**
onlar *(onlar)* **they**	onları *(onlaruh)* **them**	onların *(onlaruhn)* **theirs**

basic grammar

In Turkish there are two ways of saying 'you', informal and formal. Most of the phrases in this book use the formal. Subject pronouns are infrequently used, because the verb endings make it clear who or what the subject is.

✳ possessives

	ENDING	EXAMPLE
my	-im, -üm, -ım, -um (im, ewm, uhm, um)	evim (evim) **my house**
your	-in, -ün, -ın, -un (in, ewn, uhn, un)	evin (evin) **your house**
his/her/its	-i, -ü, -ı, -u (i, ew, uh, u)	pasaportu (pasaportu) **his/her passport**
our	-imiz, -ümüz, -ımız, -umuz (imiz, ewmewz, uhmuhz, umuz)	kızımız (kuhzuhmuhz) **our daughter**
your	-iniz, -ünüz, -ınız, -unuz (imiz, ewnewz, uhnuhz, unuz)	eşiniz (eshiniz) **your husband/wife**
their	-leri, -ları (leri, laruh)	çocukları (chojuklaruh) **their children**

If the basic word ends in a vowel:
- add an s before the 'his/her/its' endings, e.g. odası (odasuh) his/her room.
- drop the initial vowel of the possessive ending, e.g. odam (odam) my room.

To make a phrase like 'John's car', both words take endings. The possessor comes first, e.g. Ali'nin arkadaşı (alinin arkadashuh) Ali's friend

✳ adjectives

Adjectives always come before the noun, and they don't change according to the case of the noun they describe.

For comparatives the word daha *(daha)* is used before the adjective:

daha güzel *(daha gewzel)* more beautiful

daha iyi *(daha iyi)* better

For superlatives the word en *(en)* is used before the adjective:

en ucuz *(en ujuz)* cheapest

en pahalı *(en pahaluh)* most expensive

✳ verbs

Verbs are listed in dictionaries in the infinitive form. Turkish infinitives end in -mek or -mak, e.g. gitmek *(gitmek)* 'to go', çalışmak *(chaluhshmak)* 'to work'.

Turkish verbs have endings for both the tense and the subject of the verb. To use the verb in a sentence, remove the -mek/-mak ending and then add the appropriate tense and subject endings to the verb stem. In Turkish, verbs are placed at the end of a sentence.

✳ the verb 'to be'

The present tense of the verb 'to be' is formed by adding the following endings to a noun or adjective, according to the rule of vowel harmony.

PRESENT TENSE	
I am	-(y)im, -(y)üm, -(y)ım, -(y)um *([y]im, [y]ewm, [y]uhm, [y]um)*
you are (informal)	-sin, -sün, -sın, -sun *(sin, sewn, suhn, sun)*
he/she/it is	[-dir, -dür, -dır, -dur]* *(dir, dewr, duhr, dur)*
we are	-(y)iz, -(y)üz, -(y)ız, -(y)uz *([y]iz, [y]ewz, [y]uhz, [y]uz)*
you are (formal)	-siniz, -sünüz, -sınız, -sunuz *(siniz, sewnewz, suhnuhz, sunuz)*
they are	[-dir(ler), -dür(ler), -dır(lar), -dur(lar)]* *(-dir[ler], dewr[ler], duhr[lar], -dur[lar])*

* these endings are not generally used in spoken Turkish

For the negative of 'to be', the noun or adjective is unchanged and the personal endings are added to a separate word değil *(de:il)*, e.g. Öğretmen değilim *(ö:retmen de:ilim)* 'I am not a teacher'.

For questions, the noun or the adjective remains unchanged and the personal endings are added to the question endings -mi, -mü, -mı, -mu *(mi, mew, muh, mu)*, e.g. Öğretmen misiniz? *(ö:retmen misiniz)* 'Are you a teacher?'.

* present tense

The endings for the present tense if the verb ends in a consonant are: -iyor *(iyor)*, -üyor *(ewyor)*, -ıyor *(uhyor)*, -uyor *(uyor)*. If the verb ends in a vowel, it's simply -yor *(yor)*. If the verb ends in e or a, then these vowels are replaced by i and ı respectively.

SUBJECT ENDINGS		
-um	*(um)*	**I**
-sun	*(sun)*	**you** (informal)
	(none)	**he/she/it**
-uz	*(uz)*	**we**
-sunuz	*(sunuz)*	**you** (formal)
-lar	*(lar)*	**they**

* irregular verbs

There are very few irregular verbs in Turkish. Two useful ones are: gitmek *(gitmek)* 'to go' which has gid, not git, as its present tense stem, and anlamak *(anlamak)* 'to understand', which has anlı, not anla, as its stem, e.g. anlıyorum *(anluhyorum)* 'I understand'.

GITMEK		
gidiyorum	*(gidiyorum)*	**I am going**
gidiyorsun	*(gidiyorsun)*	**you are going** (informal)
gidiyor	*(gidiyor)*	**he/she/it is going**
gidiyoruz	*(gidiyoruz)*	**we are going**
gidiyorsunuz	*(gidiyorsunuz)*	**you are going**
gidiyorlar	*(gidiyorlar)*	**they are going** (formal)

To make a verb negative in the present tense, add -mi, -mü, -mı or -mu *(mi, mew, muh, mu)* to the stem before the other endings. For example, çalışmıyorum *(chaluhshmuhyorum)* 'I am not working'.

To turn a statement into a question, add -mi, -mü, -mı or -mu before the subject ending:

Salata istiyor musunuz? *(salata istiyor musunuz)* Do you want salad?

* past tense

The past tense endings are -di, -dü, -dı, -du *(di, dew, duh, du)* changing to -ti, -tü, -tı, -tu *(ti, tew, tuh, tu)* after the consonants ç, f, h, k, p, s, ş, or t.

SUBJECT ENDINGS		
-m	*(m)*	I
-n	*(n)*	you (informal)
	(none)	he/she/it
-k	*(k)*	we
-niz, -nüz, -niz, -nuz	*(niz, newz, nuhz, nuz)*	you (formal)
-ler, -lar	*(ler, lar)*	they

Çalıştım. *(chaluhshtuhm)* I worked.
Sinemaya gittik. *(sinemaya gittik)* We went to the cinema.

To form negatives, add -me or -ma *(me, ma)* before all the other endings:
Çalışmadım. *(chaluhshmaduhm)* I didn't work.
Sinemaya gitmedik. *(sinemaya gitmedik)* We didn't go to the cinema.
To turn statements into questions, add mi, mü, mı, or mu *(mi, mew, muh, mu)* at the end of the sentence:
Çalıştın mı? *(chaluhshtuhn muh)* Did you work?
Sinemaya gittiniz mi? *(sinemaya gittiniz mi)* Did you go to the cinema?

✳ the verb 'to have'

For the verb 'to have', add the possessive ending to what is possessed, and place the word var *(var)* for 'has/have' or yok *(yok)* for 'has/have not' at the end of the sentence:

kız *(kuhz)* daughter   Bir kızım var *(bir kuhzuhm var)*
                      I have a daughter.
para *(para)* money   Paramız yok *(paramuhz yok)*
                      We don't have money.

For questions, add -mı *(muh)* after var, and -mu *(mu)* after yok:
araba *(araba)* car   Arabanız var mı? *(arabanuhz var muh)*
                      Do you have a car?
havlu *(havlu)* towel   Havlu yok mu? *(temiz havlu yok mu)*
                      Aren't there any towels?

var and yok also mean 'there is/are' and 'there is/are not':
Çok tuz var. *(chok tuz var)* There is too much salt.
Odada duş yok. *(odada dush yok)* There is no shower in the room.

✳ question words

The position of question words can vary depending on what is being emphasised, but in general the question word goes before the verb.

basic grammar

English – Turkish dictionary

There's a list of **car parts** on page 60 and **parts of the body** on page 150. See also the **menu reader** on page 94, and **numbers** on page 14.

A

a, an bir *bir*
abbey manastır *manastuhr*
about *(approximately)* yaklaşık *yaklashuhk (relating to)* hakkında *hakkuhnda*
approximately yaklaşık olarak *yaklashuhk olarak*
abroad yurt dışı *yurt duhshuh*
to accept kabul etmek *kabul etmek*
accident kaza *kaza*
accommodation kalacak yer *kalajak yer*
ache ağrı *a:ruh*
across *(opposite)* karşı *karshuh*
actor erkek oyuncu *erkek oyunju*
actress bayan oyuncu *bayan oyunju*
adaptor adaptör *adaptör*
addicted bağımlı *ba:uhmluh*
address adres *adres*
admission charge kabul ücreti *kabul ewjreti*
adult yetişkin, büyük *yetishkin, bewyewk*
advance ilerleme,avans *ilerleme, avans*
 » in advance önden,peşin *önden, peshin*
advertisement, advertising reklam *reklam*
aeroplane uçak *uchak*
after -den/-dan sonra *-den / -dan sonra*
afterwards daha sonra *daha sonra*
afternoon öğleden sonra *ö:leden sonra*
afternoon performance öğleden sonra gösterisi, matinesi *ö:leden sonra gösterisi, matinesi*
aftershave traş losyonu *trash losyonu*
again tekrar *tekrar*

against karşı *karshuh*
agency acenta *ajenta*
ago önce *önje*
AIDS aids *aids*
air hava *hava*
 » by air uçakla *uchakla*
 » air mail uçak postası *uchak postasuh*
air conditioning havalandırma, klima *havalanduhrma, klima*
airport havaalanı *havaalanuh*
aisle koridor *koridor*
alarm alarm *alarm*
alarm clock çalar saat *chalar saat*
alcohol alkol *alkol*
alcoholic *(person)* alkolik *alkolik*
all hepsi *hepsi*
allergic to -e/-a/-ye/-ya alerjik *-e/-a/-ye/-ya alerzhik*
to allow izin vermek *izin vermek*
allowed izinli *izinli*
all right (OK) tamam *tamam*
almond badem *ba:dem*
along boyunca *boyunja*
already zaten *za:ten*
also hem de *hem de*
always her zaman *her zaman*
ambulance ambulans *ambulans*
American Amerikalı *amerikaluh*
amount miktar *miktar*
anaesthetic *(local)* anestetik (lokal) *anestetik (lokal) (general)* (genel) *(genel)*
and ve *ve*
angry kızgın *kuhzguhn*
animal hayvan *hayvan*

antibiotics antibiyotik *antibiyotik*

antifreeze antifiriz *antifiriz*

antique antik *antik*

any hiç *hich*

anyone kimse *kimse*

anything bir şey *bir shey*

anything else başka bir şey *bashka bir shey*

anywhere herhangi bir yer *herhangi bir yer*

apartment daire *daire*

appetite iştah *ishtah*

apple elma *elma*

to apply başvurmak *bashvurmak*

appointment randevu *randevu*

approximately yaklaşık *yaklashuhk*

arch kemer *kemer*

architect mimar *mi:mar*

area alan *alan*

arm kol *kol*

armbands *(swimming)* kolluk *kolluk*

army ordu *ordu*

to arrange düzenlemek *dewzenlemek*

arrest: under arrest tutuklu *tutuklu*

arrival varış *varuhsh*

to arrive varmak *varmak*

art sanat *sanat*

» art gallery sanat galerisi *sanat galerisi*

arthritis artrit *artrit*

artificial yapay *yapay*

artist sanatçı *sanatchuh*

as *(like)* gibi *gibi*

as far as I know bildiğim kadarıyla *bildi: im kadaruhyla*

ashtray sigara tablası *sigara tablasuh*

aspirin aspirin *aspirin*

asthma astım *astuhm*

at once hemen *hemen*

at *(the)* -de,-da,-te,-ta *-de, -da, -te, -ta*

attractive çekici *chekiji*

aubergine patlıcan *patluhjan*

aunt *(mother's sister)* teyze *teyze*
(father's sister) hala *hala*

(uncle's wife) yenge *yenge*

author yazar *yazar*

automatic otomatik *otomatik*

autumn sonbahar *sonbahar*

avocado avokado *avokado*

to avoid kaçınmak *kachuhnmak*

B

baby bebek *bebek*

baby food bebek maması *bebek mamasuh*

baby wipes ıslak mendil *ıslak mendil*

babysitter bebek bakıcısı *bebek bakuhjuhsuh*

back *(reverse side)* arka *arka*

backwards geriye *geriye*

bacon jambon *zhambon*

bad kötü *kötew*

bag çanta *chanta*

bakery fırın *fuhruhn*

balcony *(theatre etc.)* balkon *balkon*

bald kel *kel*

ball *(small)* top *top*

» *(large)* küçük,büyük *kewchewk, bewyewk*

ballet bale *bale*

ballpoint pen tükenmez kalem *tewkenmez kalem*

balloon balon *balon*

banana muz *muz*

bank banka *banka*

banknote banknot, kağıt para *banknot, ka:uht para*

bar bar *bar*

barber's berber *berber*

bargain pazarlık *pazarluhk*

basement bodrum *bodrum*

basin *(bowl)* kase *ka:se*

basket sepet *sepet*

bath banyo *banyo*

» to have a bath banyo yapmak *banyo yapmak*

bathroom banyo *banyo*

bathtub küvet *kewvet*

battery *(car)* akü *akew* (torch etc.) pil *pil*
bay koy *koy*
to **be** olmak *olmak*
beach plaj *plazh*
beans fasulye *fasulye*
  » **French/green** çalı/yeşil *chaluh/yeshil*
  » **haricot** kuru *kuru*
beard sakal *sakal*
beautiful güzel *gewzel*
because çünkü *chewnkew*
bed yatak *yatak*
bedroom yatak odası *yatak odasuh*
bee arı *aruh*
beef dana *dana*
beer bira *bira*
before önce *önje*
to **begin** başlamak *bashlamak*
beginner acemi *ajemi*
behind arka *arka*
to **believe** inanmak *inanmak*
bell zil *zil*
below aşağıda *asha:uhda*
belt kemer *kemer*
best en iyi *en iyi*
better daha iyi *daha iyi*
between arasında *arasuhnda*
bicycle bisiklet *bisiklet*
big büyük *bewyewk*
bigger daha büyük *daha bewyewk*
bill hesap *hesap*
bin çöp kutusu *chöp kutusu*
bin liner çöp torbası *chöp torbasuh*
bird kuş *kush*
birthday doğum günü *do:um gewnew*
biscuit bisküvi *biskewvi*
a bit biraz *biraz*
to **bite** ısırmak *uhsuhrmak*
bitter acı *ajuh*
black siyah *siyah*
  » **black and white (film)** siyah-beyaz
    (film) *siyah-beyaz (film)*
  » **black coffee** sütsüz kahve *sewtsewz*
    kahve
blanket battaniye *batta:niye*

bleach çamaşır suyu *chamashuhr suyu*
to **bleed** kanamak *kanamak*
blind kör *kör*
to **blister** su toplamak *su toplamak*
blonde sarışın *saruhshuhn*
blood kan *kan*
blouse bluz *bluz*
blue mavi *ma:vi*
to **board** binmek *binmek*
boarding card biniş kartı *binish kartuh*
boat vapur, tekne *vapur, tekne*
boat trip tekne gezisi *tekne gezisi*
body vücut *vewjut*
to **boil** kaynamak *kaynamak*
  » **boiled egg** kaynamış yumurta
    kaynamuhsh yumurta
boiler su ısıtıcısı *su uhsuhtuhjuhsuh*
bone kemik *kemik*
book kitap *kitap*
to **book** ayırtmak *ayuhrtmak*
booking rezervasyon *rezervasyon*
booking office bilet gişesi *bilet gishesi*
booklet broşür, kitapçık *broshewr,*
    kitapchuhk
bookshop kitapçı *kitapchuh*
border *(frontier)* hudut *hudut*
boring sıkıcı *suhkuhjuh*
both ikisi *ikisi*
bottle şişe *shishe*
bottle opener açacak *achajak*
bowl kase *ka:se*
box *(theatre)* loca *loja*
boy oğlan *o:lan*
boyfriend erkek arkadaş *erkek arkadash*
bra sütyen *sewtyen*
bracelet bilezik *bilezik*
brake fren *fren*
brand marka *marka*
brand new yepyeni *yepyeni*
bread ekmek *ekmek*
  » **wholemeal bread** kepekli ekmek
    kepekli ekmek
to **break** kırmak *kuhrmak*
to **break down** bozmak *bozmak*

breakfast kahvaltı *kahvaltuh*
to breathe nefes almak *nefes almak*
bride gelin *gelin*
bridegroom damat *da:mat*
bridge köprü *köprew*
briefcase evrak çantası *evrak chantasuh*
bright (colour) canlı, parlak *janluh, parlak*
(light) aydınlık *ayduhnluhk*
to bring getirmek *getirmek*
British İngiliz *ingiliz*
broken kırık *kuhruhk*
bronchitis bronşit *bronshit*
bronze bronz *bronz*
brown kahverengi *kahverengi*
brown sugar esmer şeker *esmer sheker*
bruise morluk *morluk*
brush fırça *fuhrcha*
buffet yemek *yemek*
to build inşa etmek *insha etmek*
building bina *bina*
bulb (light) ampul *ampul*
bumper (car) çamurluk *chamurluk*
burn yanık *yanuhk*
to burn yakmak *yakmak*
burnt yanmış *yanmuhsh*
bus otobüs *otobews*
  » by bus otobüsle *otobewsle*
business iş *ish*
  » business trip iş gezisi *ish gezisi*
  » on business iş gezisinde *ish gezisinde*
businessman/woman iş adamı, iş kadını *ish adamuh, ish kaduhnuh*
bus station otogar *otogar*
bus stop otobüs durağı *otobews dura:uh*
busy meşgul *meshgul*
but ama *ama*
butane gas bütan gaz *bewtan gaz*
butcher's kasap *kasap*
butter tereyağı *tereya:uh*
button düğme *dew:me*
to buy almak *almak*
by ile *ile*

C

cabbage lahana *lahana*
cabin kabin *kabin*
cable car teleferik *teleferik*
café pastane, kafe *pasta:ne, kafe*
cake kek *kek*
cake shop pastane *pastane*
to call (phone) telefon etmek *telefon etmek*
to call çağırmak *cha:uhrmak*
  » to be called (he/she/it) ismi *ismi*
calm sakin *sa:kin*
camcorder video kamera *video kamera*
camera fotoğraf makinası *foto:raf makinasuh*
camomile tea papatya çayı *papatya chayuh*
to camp kamp yapmak *kamp yapmak*
camp bed kamp yatağı *kamp yata:uh*
camping gas kamping gaz *kamping gaz*
camping kamping *kamping*
campsite kamp yeri *kamp yeri*
can (tin) kutu *kutu*
can opener konserve açacağı *konserve achaja:uh*
to cancel iptal etmek *iptal etmek*
cancer kanser *kanser*
candle mum *mum*
canoe kano *kano*
capital (city) başkent *bashkent*
car araba *araba*
  » by car arabayla *arabayla*
car hire kiralık araba *kira:luhk araba*
carafe cam sürahi *jam sewrahi*
caravan karavan *karavan*
career meslek, kariyer *meslek, kariyer*
careful dikkatli *dikkatli*
car park otopark, park yeri *otopark, park yeri*
carriage (train) vagon *vagon*
carrier bag torba *torba*
carrot havuç *havuch*
to carry taşımak *tashuhmak*
carton karton (kutu) *karton (kutu)*
car wash araba yıkama *araba yuhkama*

cash nakit *nakit*
» to pay cash nakit ödemek *nakit ödemek*
cash desk vezne *vezne*
cashpoint bankamatik *bankamatik*
castle kale *kale*
cat kedi *kedi*
to catch yakalamak *yakalamak*
cathedral katedral *katedral*
Catholic katolik *katolik*
CD CD *cd*
CD-Rom CD-rom *cd-rom*
centimetre santimetre *santimetre*
central merkezi *merkezi*
central heating merkezi ısıtma *merkezi uhsuhtma*
centre merkez *merkez*
century yüzyıl *yewzuyhl*
CEO (chief executive officer) şef genel müdür *shef genel mewdewr*
cereal kornfleks *kornfleks*
certificate sertifika *sertifika*
chain zincir *zinjir*
chair sandalye *sandalye*
chair lift koltuklu teleferik *koltuklu teleferik*
chalet dağ evi *da: evi*
champagne şampanya *shampanya*
championship şampiyonluk *shampiyonluk*
change (coins) bozuk para *bozuk para*
to change (clothes) üstünü değişmek *ewstewnew de:ishmek* (money) para bozdurmak *para bozdurmak* (trains) aktarma yapmak *aktarma yapmak*
changing room giyinme kabini *giyinme kabini*
chapel küçük kilise, mabet *kewchewk kilise, ma:bet*
cheap ucuz *ujuz*
checkout (till) kasa *kasa*
checked (pattern) kareli *kareli*
to check-in kayıt yaptırmak *kayuht yaptuhrmak*

Cheers! şerefe! *sherefe*
cheese peynir *peynir*
chemist eczane *ejza:ne*
cheque çek *chek*
chest göğüs *gö:ews*
chestnut kestane *kesta:ne*
chewing gum sakız *sakuhz*
chicken tavuk *tavuk*
chicken pox su çiçeği *su chije:i*
child çocuk *chojuk*
children çocuklar *chojuklar*
china porselen *porselen*
chips cips *jips*
chocolate çikolata *chikolata*
to choose seçmek *sechmek*
Christian Hiristiyan *huhristiyan*
Christian name vaftizde verilen ad *vaftizde verilen aduh*
Christmas Noel *noel*
Christmas Day Noel günü *noel gewnew*
Christmas Eve Noel arifesi *noel arifesi*
church kilise *kilise*
cigar puro *puro*
cigarette sigara *sigara*
cinema sinema *sinema*
circle (in theatre) balkon *balkon*
circus sirk *sirk*
city şehir *shehir*
class sınıf *suhnuhf*
classical music klasik müzik *klasik mewzik*
to clean temizlemek *temizlemek*
clean temiz *temiz*
clever akıllı *akuhlluh*
cliff uçurum *uchurum*
climate iklim *iklim*
to climb tırmanmak *tuhrmanmak*
clinic klinik *klinik*
cloakroom vestiyer *vestiyer*
clock saat *saat*
close (by) yakın *yakuhn*
to close kapamak *kapamak*
closed kapalı *kapaluh*

clothes elbiseler *elbiseler*
cloudy bulutlu *bulutlu*
club kulüp *kulewp*
clutch debriyaj *debriyazh*
coach (uzun yol için) otobüs *(uzun yol ichin) otobews*
coast sahil *sa:hil*
coat palto *palto*
coat-hanger askı *askuh*
cocktail kokteyl *kokteyl*
coffee kahve *kahve*
coin madeni para *ma:deni para*
cocoa kakao *kakao*
cod morina balığı *morina baluh:uh*
cold soğuk *so:uk*
 » to have a cold nezle olmak *nezle olmak*
collar yaka *yaka*
colleague meslektaş *meslektash*
college fakülte *fakewlte*
colour renk *renk*
colour-blind renk körü *renk körew*
comb tarak *tarak*
to come gelmek *gelmek*
to come back geri dönmek *geri dönmek*
to come in girmek *girmek*
 come in! girin *girin*
to come off kopmak *kopmak*
comedy komedi *komedi*
comfortable rahat *rahat*
comic (magazine) resimli mizah dergisi *resimli mizah dergisi*
commercial ticari *tija:ri*
common (usual) genel *genel* (shared) yaygın *yayguhn*
communion ortak *ortak*
communism komünizm *komewnizm*
commission komisyon *komisyon*
company şirket *shirket*
compared with göre *göre*
compartment kompartman *kompartman*
to complain şikayet etmek *shikayet etmek*
complaint şikayet *shikayet*
complete tamamlamak *tamamlamak*

complicated karmaşık *karmashuhk*
compulsory zorunlu *zorunlu*
composer besteci *besteji*
computer bilgisayar *bilgisayar*
computer operator bilgisayar operatörü *bilgisayar operatörew*
concert konser *konser*
concert hall konser salonu *konser salonu*
concession itiraf *itiraf*
concussion çarpışma *charpuhshma*
condition durum *durum*
conditioner (hair) yumuşatıcı *yumushatuhjuh*
condom prezervatif *prezervatif*
connection bağlantı *ba:lantuh*
conference konferans *:konferans*
to confirm doğrulamak *do:rulamak*
conjunctivitis konjonktivit *konzhonktivit*
conservation koruma *koruma*
conservative muhafazakar *muhafazakar*
constipation kabız *kabuhz*
consulate konsolosluk *konsolosluk*
contact lens kontak lens *kontak lens*
contact lens cleaner kontak lens temizleyici *kontak lens temizleyiji*
contagious bulaşıcı *bulashuhjuh*
continent kıta *kuhta*
contraceptive gebeliği önleyici *gebeli:i önleyiji*
to continue devam etmek *devam etmek*
convenient uygun *uygun*
to cook pişirmek *pishirmek*
cooked pişmiş *pishmish*
cooker ocak *ojak*
cool serin *serin*
copy kopya *kopya*
cork mantar *mantar*
corkscrew tirbuşon *tirbushon*
corner (outside) köşe *köshe*
correct doğru *do:ru*
corridor koridor *koridor*
cosmetics makyaj malzemesi *makyaj malzemesi*
to cost tutmak *tutmak*

cot bebek yatağı *bebek yata:uh*
cottage kulübe *kulewbe*
cotton *(material)* pamuklu *pamuklu*
   (thread) iplik *iplik*
cotton wool pamuk *pamuk*
couchette kuşet *kushet*
cough öksürük *öksewrewk*
to count saymak *saymak*
country ülke *ewlke*
   » in the country ülkede *ewlkede*
countryside kırsal bölge *kuhrsal bölge*
couple (pair) çift *chift*
courgette kabak *kabak*
course *(lessons)* ders *ders*
court *(law)* mahkeme *mahkeme (tennis)*
   kort *kort*
cousin kuzen *kuzen*
cover *(lid)* kapak *kapak*
cow inek *inek*
crab yengeç *yengech*
cramp kramp *kramp*
cream *(food)* krema *krema (lotion)* krem
   krem (colour) krem rengi *krem rengi*
credit card kredi kartı *kredi kartuh*
cricket kriket *kriket*
crisps gevrek *gevrek*
cross haç *hach*
to cross geçmek *gechmek*
cross-country skiing kayaklı koşu
   kayakluh koshu
crossing dörtyol (ağzı) *dörtyol (a:zuh)*
crossroad kavşak *kavshak*
crowd kalabalık *kalabaluhk*
crowded kalabalık *kalabaluhk*
crown taç *tach*
cruise deniz yolculuğu *deniz yoljulu:u*
crutch koltuk değneği *koltuk de:ne:i*
to cry ağlamak *a:lamak*
crystal kristal *kristal*
cucumber salatalık *salataluhk*
cup fincan *finjan*
cupboard dolap *dolap*
cure tedavi *teda:vi*
to cure tedavi etmek *tedavi etmek*

curler *(hair)* bigudi *bigudi*
curly kıvırcık *kuhvuhrjuhk*
curry köri *köri*
current *(electricity)* akım *akuhm*
curtain perde *perde*
curve dönemeç, eğim *dönemech, e:im*
cushion yastık *yastuhk*
customs gümrük *gewmrewk*
customer müşteri *mewshteri*
cut kesik *kesik*
to cut kesmek *kesmek*
cycling bisiklete binmek *bisiklete binmek*
cyclist bisikletçi *bisikletchi*

D

daily günlük *gewnlewk*
dairy products süt ürünleri *sewt*
   ewrewnleri
damage hasar *hasar*
to damage hasar vermek *hasar vermek*
damp rutubetli *rutubetli*
to dance dans etmek *dans etmek*
danger tehlike *tehlike*
dangerous tehlikeli *tehlikeli*
dark *(colour)* koyu *koyu (light)* karanlık
   karanluhk
darling sevgili *sevgili*
date *(day)* tarih *tarih (fruit)* hurma *hurma*
daughter kız çocuk *kuhz chojuk*
daughter-in-law gelin *gelin*
day gün *gewn*
day after tomorrow öbür gün *öbewr*
   gewn
day before yesterday ertesi gün *ertesi*
   gewn
day after/before sonraki, önceki gün
   sonraki, önjeki gewn
dead ölü *ölew*
dead end çıkmaz yol *chuhkmaz yol*
deaf sağır *sa:uhr*
dear *(loved)* sevgili *sevgili (expensive)*
   pahalı *pahaluh*
death ölüm *ölewm*
debt borç *borch*

decaffeinated coffee kafeinsiz kahve *kafeinsiz kahve*

deck güverte *gewverte*

deckchair şezlong *shezlong*

to decide karar vermek *karar vermek*

to declare açıklamak *achuhklamak*

deep derin *derin*

deer geyik *geyik*

defect defo *defo*

defective hatalı *hataluh*

definitely kesinlikle *kesinlikle*

defrost eritmek *eritmek*

degree *(temperature)* derece *dereje* *(university)* lisans *lisans*

delay gecikme *gejikme*

delicate hassas *hassas*

delicatessen şarküteri *sharkewteri*

delicious lezzetli *lezzetli*

delighted hoşnut *hoshnut*

to deliver teslim etmek *teslim etmek*

delivery teslim *teslim*

demonstration gösteri *gösteri*

denim kot kumaş *kot kumash*

dentist dişçi *dishchi*

dentures takma diş *takma dish*

deodorant deodorant *deodorant*

to depart hareket etmek *hareket etmek*

department *(in shop)*reyon *reyon*

department store mağaza *ma:aza*

departure kalkış *kalkuhsh*

departure lounge gidiş salonu *gidish salonu*

deposit depozito *depozito*

depth derinlik *derinlik*

to describe tarif etmek *ta:rif etmek*

description tarif *ta:rif*

desert çöl *chöl*

design desen *desen*

designer çizimci *chizimji*

dessert tatlı *tatluh*

destination gidiş yeri *gidish yeri*

detergent deterjan *deterzhan*

to develop gelişmek *gelishmek*

diabetes şeker hastalığı *sheker hastaluh:uh*

diabetic şeker hastası *sheker hastasuh*

to dial çevirmek *chevirmek*

dialling code kod numarası *kod numarasuh*

dialling tone çevir sinyali *chevir sinyali*

diamond pırlanta *puhrlanta*

diarrhoea ishal, diyare *ishal, diyare*

dice zar *zar*

dictionary sözlük *sözlewk*

to die ölmek *ölmek*

died öldü *öldew*

diesel dizel *dizel*

diet rejim *rezhim*

different(ly) değişik *de:ishik*

difficult zor *zor*

digital dijital *dizhital*

digital camera dijital kamera *dzhijital kamera*

dining room yemek odası *yemek odasuh*

dinner akşam yemeği *aksham yeme:i*

dinner jacket smokin *smokin*

diplomat diplomat *diplomat*

direct *(train)* direkt *direkt*

direction yön, istikamet *yön, istika:met*

directory telefon rehberi *telefon rehberi*

dirty kirli *kirli*

disabled özürlü *özewrlew*

disappointment hayal kırıklığı *hayal kuhruhkluh:uh*

disc *(computer)* disk *disk*

disco diskotek *diskotek*

discount indirim *indirim*

dish yemek *yemek*

dishwasher bulaşık makinası *bulashuhk makinasuh*

disinfectant dezenfektan *dezenfektan*

dislocated yerinden çıkmış *yerinden chuhkmuhsh*

disposable atılabilir *atuhlabilir*

disposable camera tek kullanımlık fotoğraf makinası *tek kullanuhmluhk foto:raf makinasuh*

distance mesafe *mesa:fe*

district bölge *bölge*

to disturb rahatsız etmek *rahatsuhz etmek*
to dive dalmak *dalmak*
  diversion sapma *sapma*
  diving dalış *daluhsh*
  diving board atlama tahtası *atlama tahtasuh*
  divorced boşanmış *boshanmuhsh*
  DIY yapı market *yapuh market*
  dizzy baş dönmesi *bash dönmesi*
to do yapmak *yapmak*
  dock rıhtım *ruhhtuhm*
  doctor doktor *doktor*
  document belge *belge*
  dog köpek *köpek*
  doll bebek *bebek*
  dollar dolar *dolar*
  dome kubbe *kubbe*
  donkey eşek *eshek*
  door (train, car) kapı *kapuh*
  double çift *chift*
  double bed iki kişilik yatak *iki kishilik yatak*
  down aşağı *asha:uh*
to download yüklemek *yewklemek*
  downstairs aşağı kat *asha:uh kat*
  drain oluk *oluk*
  draught beer fıçı bira *fuhchuh bira*
to draw çizmek *chizmek*
  drawer çekmece *chekmeje*
  drawing resim *resim*
  dreadful korkunç *korkunch*
  dress elbise *elbise*
to dress, get dressed giyinmek *giyinmek*
  dressing (medical) sargı *sarguh*
  (salad) sos *sos*
  drink içki *ichki*
to drink içmek *ichmek*
  drinking (water) içme suyu *ichme suyu*
to drive araba kullanmak *araba kullanmak*
  driving licence ehliyet *ehliyet*
  drowsiness uyuşukluk *uyushukluk*
  drug ilaç *ilach*
  drug addict madde bağımlısı *madde ba: uhmluhsuh*

dry kuru *kuru* (wine) sek *sek*
dry-cleaner's kuru temizlemeci *kuru temizlemeji*
dubbed dublajlı *dublajluh*
dummy (baby's) emzik *emzik*
during sırasında *suhrasuhnda*
dust toz *toz*
dustbin çöp kutusu *chöp kutusu*
dusty tozlu *tozlu*
duty (tax) gümrük *gewmrewk*
duty-free gümrük vergisiz *gewmrewk vergisiz*
duvet yorgan *yorgan*
DVD dvd *dvd*
DVD-player dvd-çalar *dvd-chalar*
dyslexia disleksi *disleksi*
dyslexic disleksik *disleksik*

E

each her *her*
ear infection kulak enfeksiyonu *kulak enfeksiyonu*
early erken *erken*
to earn kazanmak *kazanmak*
  earring küpe *kewpe*
  earth dünya *dewnya*
  east doğu *do:u*
  eastern doğulu *do:ulu*
  Easter paskalya *paskalya*
  easy kolay *kolay*
to eat yemek *yemek*
  Economics ekonomi *ekonomi*
  economy ekonomi *ekonomi*
  edible yenebilir *yenebilir*
  effort çaba *chaba*
  egg yumurta *yumurta*
  eggs yumurtalar *yumurtalar*
  either... or... ya... ya *ya... ya*
  election seçim *sechim*
  electrician elektrikçi *elektrikchi*
  electricity elektrik *elektrik*
  electronic elektronik *elektronik*
  email eposta *eposta*
to email eposta göndermek *eposta*

göndermek

to embark *(boat)* binmek *binmek*

embassy büyükelçilik *bewyewkelchilik*

emergency acil *ajil*

empty boş *bosh*

to empty boşaltmak *boshaltmak*

end son *son*

to end bitmek *bitmek*

energy enerji *enerji*

engaged *(to be married)* nişanlı *nishanluh*
(occupied) dolu *dolu*

England İngiltere *ingiltere*

English İngilizce *ingilizje*

to enjoy hoşlanmak *hoshlanmak*

enough yeter *yeter*

to enter girmek *girmek*

entertainment eğlence *e:lenje*

entrance giriş *girish*

envelope zarf *zarf*

environment çevre *chevre*

environmentally friendly çevre dostu
chevre dostu

epilepsy epilepsi *epilepsi*

epileptic epilepsili, saralı *epilepsili,
saraluh*

equal eşit *eshit*

equipment malzeme *malzeme*

especially özellikle *özellikle*

essential şart *shart*

estate agent emlakçı *emlakchuh*

even *(including)* bile *bile* *(not odd)* çift
chift

evening akşam *aksham*

every her *her*

everyone herkes *herkes*

everything her şey *her shey*

everywhere her yer *her yer*

exact(ly) tam *tam*

examination imtihan, sınav *imtihan,
suhnav*

exams imtihanlar, sınavlar *imtihanlar,
suhnavlar*

example örnek *örnek*

» for example örneğin *örne:in*

excellent harika *ha:rika*

except dışında *duhshuhnda*

excess baggage fazla bagaj *fazla bagazh*

to exchange *(money)* para bozdurmak *para
bozdurmak*

exchange rate kur *kur*

excited heyecanlı *heyejanluh*

exciting heyecanlı *heyejanluh*

excursion gezi *gezi*

excuse me affedersiniz *affedersiniz*

exercise jimnastik *zhimnastik*

exhibition sergi *sergi*

exit çıkış *chuhkuhsh*

to expect beklemek *beklemek*

expensive pahalı *pahaluh*

experience deneyim *deneyim*

experiment deney *deney*

expert uzman *uzman*

to explain anlatmak *anlatmak*

explosion patlama *patlama*

export ihraç *ihrach*

to export ihraç etmek *ihrach etmek*

exposure *(photo)* poz *poz*

express ekspres *ekspres*

extension cable uzatma kablosu *uzatma
kablosu*

external dış *duhsh*

extra fazladan *fazladan*

to extract çıkarmak *chuhkarmak*

eyebrow kaş *kash*

eyelash kirpik *kirpik*

eyeliner göz kalemi *göz kalemi*

eyeshadow göz boyası *göz boyasuh*

F

fabric kumaş *kumash*

face yüz *yewz*

face cream yüz kremi *yewz kremi*

face powder pudra *pudra*

facilities olanaklar *olanaklar*

fact gerçek *gerchek*

» in fact gerçekten *gerchekten*

factory fabrika *fabrika*

to fail *(exam/text)* kalmak *kalmak*

failure başarısızlık *basharuhsuhzluhk*
to faint bayılmak *bayuhlmak*
fair (haired) sarışın *saruhshuhn*
fair fuar *fuar*
fairly oldukça *oldukcha*
faith inanç *inanch*
fake sahte *sahte*
to fall düşmek *dewshmek*
false sahte *sahte*
familiar aşina *a:shina*
family aile *aile*
famous ünlü *ewnlew*
fan (air) yelpaze *yelpa:ze* (supporter) taraftar *taraftar*
fantastic harika *harika*
far (away) uzak *uzak*
fare bilet parası *bilet parasuh*
farm çiftlik *chiftlik*
farmer çiftçi *chiftchi*
fashion moda *moda*
fashionable/in fashion moda *moda*
fast hızlı *huhzluh*
fat yağ *ya:*
fatal öldürücü *öldewrewjew*
father baba *baba*
father-in-law kayınpeder *kayuhnpeder*
fault defo *defo*
faulty defolu *defolu*
favourite favori *favori*
fax faks *faks*
feather tüy *tewy*
to be fed up bıkmak *buhkmak*
fee ücret *ewjret*
to feed yedirmek *yedirmek*
female, feminine dişi *dishi*
ferry vapur *vapur*
festival festival *festival*
to fetch gidip getirmek *gidip getirmek*
fever ateş *atesh*
few az *az*
fiancé(e) nişanlı *nishanluh*
fibre lif *lif*
field tarla *tarla*
fig incir *injir*

to fight kavga etmek *kavga etmek*
file (documents) dosya *dosya* (computer) dosya *dosya* (nail/DIY) törpü *törpew*
to fill doldurmak *doldurmak*
to fill up (petrol) doldurmak *doldurmak*
filling dolgu *dolgu*
film film *film* (camera) film *film*
film star film yıldızı *film yuhlduhzuh*
filter filtre *filtre*
finance finans *finans*
to find bulmak *bulmak*
fine (OK) iyi *iyi* (penalty) ceza *jeza* (weather) güzel *gewzel*
finger parmak *parmak*
finish bitirmek *bitirmek*
fire ateş *atesh*
fire brigade itfaiye *itfaiye*
fire extinguisher yangın söndürücü *yanguhn söndewrewjew*
firewood odun *odun*
fireworks havai fişek *havai fishek*
firm (company) firma *firma*
first birinci, ilk *birinji, ilk*
» first aid ilk yardım *ilk yarduhm*
» first aid kit ilk yardım çantası *ilk yarduhm chantasuh*
fish balık *baluhk*
to fish/go fishing balık tutmak, balık tutmaya gitmek *baluhk tutmak, baluhk tutmaya gitmek*
fishing rod olta *olta*
fishmonger's balıkçı *baluhkchuh*
fit (healthy) sağlıklı *sa:luhkluh*
to fit uymak *uymak*
» that fits you well size iyi uydu *size iyi uydu*
fitting room soyunma odası *soyunma odasuh*
to fix (mend) tamir etmek *tamir etmek*
fizzy köpüklü *köpewklew*
flag bayrak *bayrak*
flash (camera) flaş *flash*
flat (apartment) daire *daire*
flat (level) düz *dewz* (empty battery)

boş *bosh*

flavour tad *tad*

flea market bit pazarı *bit pazaruh*

flight uçuş *uchush*

flippers palet *palet*

floor yer *yer*

» **ground floor** zemin kat *zemin kat*

» **on the first floor** birinci katta *birinji katta*

flour un *un*

flower çiçek *chichek*

flu/influenza grip *grip*

fluent akıcı *akuhjuh*

fluid sıvı *suhvuh*

fly sinek *sinek*

fly spray sinek ilacı *sinek ilajuh*

to **fly** uçmak *uchmak*

fog sis *sis*

foggy sisli *sisli*

foil folyo *folyo*

folk music halk müziği *halk mewzi:i*

to **follow** izlemek *izlemek*

following (next) izleyen *izleyen*

food besin *besin*

food poisoning besin zehirlenmesi *besin zehirlenmesi*

foot ayak *ayak*

» **on foot** yürüyerek *yewrewyerek*

football futbol *futbol*

footpath patika *patika*

for için *ichin*

forbidden yasak *yasak*

foreign yabancı *yabanjuh*

foreigner yabancı *yabanjuh*

forest orman *orman*

to **forget** unutmak *unutmak*

to **forgive** affetmek *affetmek*

fork çatal *chatal*

form form *form*

fortnight on beş gün *on besh gewn*

fortress hisar *hisar*

forward ileri *ileri*

forwarding address gideceği adres *gideje:i adres*

foundation (make-up) fondöten *fondöten*

fountain çeşme *cheshme*

fox tilki *tilki*

foyer giriş *girish*

fracture kırık *kuhruhk*

fragile kırılacak eşya *kuhruhlajak eshya*

frankly açıkcası *achuhkjasuh*

free (available/unoccupied) serbest *serbest*

free of charge ücretsiz *ewjretsiz*

freedom özgürlük *özgewrlewk*

to **freeze** dondurmak *dondurmak*

freezer derin dondurucu *derin donduruju*

French Fransız *fransuhz*

frequent sık *suhk*

fresh taze *taze*

fridge buzdolabı *buzdolabuh*

fried kızarmış *kuhzarmuhsh*

friend arkadaş *arkadash*

frightened korkmuş *korkmush*

frog kurbağa *kurba:a*

from -den, -dan, -ten, -tan *-den, -dan, -ten, -tan*

front ön *ön*

» **in front of** önünde *önewnde*

frontier hudut *hudut*

frost don *don*

frozen donmuş *donmush*

fruit meyve *meyve*

to **fry** kızartmak *kuhzartmak*

frying pan tava *tava*

fuel yakıt *yakuht*

full dolu *dolu*

full board tam pansiyon *tam pansiyon*

full up dolu *dolu*

to have **fun** eğlenmek *e:lenmek*

» **it was fun** eğlenceliydi *e:lenjeliydi*

to **function** çalışmak *chaluhshmak*

funeral cenaze töreni *jena:ze töreni*

funfair lunapark *lunapark*

funny (amazing) komik *komik* (peculiar) garip *garip*

fur kürk *kewrk*

furniture mobilya *mobilya*

further on daha ileri *daha ileri*

fuse sigorta *sigorta*

fusebox sigorta kutusu *sigorta kutusu*

G

gallery galeri *galeri*

gambling kumar *kumar*

game oyun *oyun*

gangway geçit *gechit*

garage *(for repairs)* tamirhane *tamirhane* *(car parking)* garaj *garazh*

garden bahçe *bahche*

garlic sarımsak *saruhmsak*

gas gaz *gaz*

gas bottle/cylinder gaz tüpü *gaz tewpew*

gate *(airport)* kapı *kapuh*

gay *(homosexual)* eşcinsel *eshjinsel*

gear *(in car)* vites *vites*

gear box vites kutusu *vites kutusu*

gel *(hair)* saç jölesi *sach zhölesi*

general genel *genel*

 » **in general** genellikle *genellikle*

general practitioner, GP pratisyen hekim *pratisyen hekim*

generous cömert *jömert*

gentleman/men bey *bey*

genuine gerçek *gerchek*

to get off inmek *inmek*

to get off *(bus)* inmek *inmek*

to get on binmek *binmek*

to get through *(phone)* bağlamak *ba:lamak*

gift hediye *hediye*

gin cin *jin*

girl kız *kuhz*

girlfriend kız arkadaş *kuhz arkadash*

to give vermek *vermek*

to give way yol vermek *yol vermek*

glass bardak *bardak*

glasses gözlük *gözlewk*

global warming küresel ısınma *kewresel uhsuhnma*

gloves eldiven *eldiven*

glue yapıştırıcı *yapuhshtuhruhjuh*

gluten-free glütensiz *glewtensiz*

to go gitmek *gitmek*

to go away uzaklaşmak *uzaklashmak*

to go down aşağı inmek *asha:uh inmek*

to go in girmek *girmek*

to go out çıkmak *chuhkmak*

 » **let's go!** gidelim *gidelim*

goal gol *gol*

goat keçi *kechi*

God Allah *allah*

goggles *(safety gear)* koruyucu gözlük *koruyuju gözlewk*

goggles *(diving)* dalgıç gözlüğü *dalguhch gözlew:ew*

gold altın *altuhn*

golf golf *golf*

golf clubs golf kulübü *golf kulewbew*

golf course golf sahası *golf sahası*

good iyi *iyi*

 » **good day** iyi günler *iyi gewnler*

 » **good evening** iyi akşamlar *iyi akshamlar*

 » **good morning** günaydın *gewnayduhn*

 » **good night** iyi geceler *iyi gejeler*

goodbye *(if you are leaving)* allahaısmarladık *alasmaladuhk* *(if you are staying)* güle güle *gewle gewle*

government hükümet *hewkewmet*

gramme gram *gram*

grammar gramer *gramer*

grandchild torun *torun*

granddaughter kız torun *kuhz torun*

grandfather büyükbaba *bewyewkbaba*

grandmother *(maternal)* anneanne *anneanne (paternal)* babaanne *babaanne*

grandson erkek torun *erkek torun*

grandstand tribün *tribewn*

grape üzüm *ewzewm*

grapefruit greyfurt *greyfurt*

grass çim *chim*

greasy yağlı *ya:luh*

great! çok iyi! *chok iyi!*

green *(environmentally aware)* çevre

dostu *chevre dostu*
greengrocer's manav *manav*
to greet selamlamak *selamlamak*
grey gri *gri*
grilled ızgara *uhzgara*
grocer's bakkal *bakkal*
ground *(football)* saha *saha*
ground floor zemin kat *zemin kat*
group grup *grup*
guarantee garanti *garanti*
guest misafir *misa:fir*
guest house pansiyon *pansiyon*
guide *(person)* rehber *rehber*
guided tour rehberli tur *rehberli tur*
guidebook rehber *rehber*
guilty suçlu *suchlu*
guitar gitar *gitar*
gun silah *silah*

H

hail dolu *dolu*
hair saç *sach*
hairbrush saç fırçası *sach fuhrchasuh*
haircut saç kesimi *sach kesimi*
hairdresser kuaför *kuaför*
hairdryer saç kurutma makinası *sach kurutma makinasuh*
hairspray saç spreyi *sach spreyi*
half yarım *yaruhm*
 » half an hour yarım saat *yaruhm saat*
 » half board yarım pansiyon *yaruhm pansiyon*
 » half past... ...buçuk *...buchuk*
 » half price/fare yarı fiyat *yaruh fiyat*
hamburger hamburger *hamburger*
hammer çekiç *chekich*
hand luggage el bagajı *el bagajuh*
hand made el yapımı *el yapuhmuh*
hand bag çanta *chanta*
handkerchief mendil *mendil*
handle sap *sap* *(door)* kapı kolu *kapuh kolu*
to hang up *(telephone)* kapatmak *kapatmak*
hangover akşamdan kalma *akshamdan*

kalma
to happen olmak *olmak*
happy mutlu *mutlu*
harbour liman *liman*
hard sert *sert (difficult)* zor *zor*
hard drive *(computer)* sabit disk *sabit disk*
hard shoulder banket *banket*
hardware shop nalburiye *nalburiye*
to hate nefret etmek *nefret etmek*
hay saman *saman*
hay fever saman nezlesi *saman nezlesi*
he o *o*
headache başağrısı *basha:ruhsuh*
headlight far *far*
headphones kulaklık *kulakluhk*
to heal iyileşmek *iyileshmek*
health sağlık *sa:luhk*
healthy sağlıklı *sa:luhkluh*
to hear duymak *duymak*
hearing aid işitme cihazı *ishitme jihazuh*
heart attack kalp krizi *kalp krizi*
heat sıcaklık *suhjakluhk*
heater ısıtıcı *uhsuhtuhjuh*
heating kalorifer *kalorifer*
heaven cennet *jennet*
heavy ağır *a:uhr*
heel *(shoe)* topuk *topuk*
height yükseklik *yewkseklik*
helicopter helikopter *helikopter*
hell cehennem *jehennem*
hello merhaba *merhaba*
helmet kask *kask*
help yardım *yarduhm*
help! imdat! *imdat*
to help yardım etmek *yarduhm etmek*
her onun *onun*
herb ot *ot*
herbal tea bitki çayı *bitki chayuh*
here burada *burada*
here is burada *burada*
hers onun, onunki *onun, onunki*
high yüksek *yewksek*
high chair bebek sandalyesi *bebek sandalyesi*

to hijack kaçırmak *kachuhrmak*
hiking dağ yürüyüşü *da: yewrewyewshew*
hill tepe *tepe*
him onu *onu*
Hindu Hintli *hintli*
to hire kiralamak *kira:lamak*
his onun *onun*
history tarih *ta:rih*
to hitchhike otostop yapmak *otostop yapmak*
HIV HIV *hiv*
　》 HIV positive HIV pozitif *hiv pozitif*
hobby hobi *hobi*
to hold tutmak *tutmak* (meeting) düzenlemek *dewzenlemek*
hole delik *delik*
holiday tatil *ta:til*
　》 on holiday tatilde *ta:tilde*
holy kutsal *kutsal*
home ev *ev*
　》 at home evde *evde*
to go home eve gitmek *eve gitmek*
homemade ev yapımı *ev yapuhmuh*
homeopathic homeopatik *homeopatik*
to be homesick vatan veya ev hasreti çekmek *vatan veya ev hasreti chekmek*
homosexual eşcinsel *eshjinsel*
honest dürüst *dewrewst*
honeymoon balayı *balayuh*
to hope ummak *ummak*
　》 I hope so umarım *umaruhm*
horrible çok kötü *chok kötew*
horse at *at*
horse riding ata binmek *ata binmek*
hose hortum *hortum*
hospital hastane *hast:ane*
host ev sahibi *ev sa:hibi*
hot sıcak *suhjak* (spicy) acı *ajuh*
hotel otel *otel*
hour saat *saat*
house ev *ev*
housework ev işi *ev ishi*
how? nasıl? *nasuhl*
　》 how far? ne kadar uzak? *ne kadar uzak*

　》 how long? ne kadar (süre)? *ne kadar (sewre)*
　》 how many? kaç? *kach*
　》 how much? ne kadar? *ne kadar*
　》 how much does it cost? ne kadar?, kaça? *ne kadar, kacha*
human insan *insan*
human being insanoğlu *insano:lu*
hungry aç *ach*
to hunt avlanmak *avlanmak*
hurry: to be in a hurry acele etmek *ajele etmek*
to hurt incitmek *injitmek*
　》 it hurts ağrıyor *a:ruhyor*
husband koca *koja*
hut kulübe *kulewbe*
hygienic hijyenik *hizhyenik*

I

I ben *ben*
ice (on roads) buz *buz*
ice cream dondurma *dondurma*
　》 ice cream parlour dondurma salonu *dondurma salonu*
ice cube buz *buz*
ice rink buz pateni pisti *buz pateni pisti*
iced (coffee) buzlu *buzlu*
icy buzlu *buzlu*
idea fikir *fikir*
if eğer *e:er*
ill hasta *hasta*
illness hastalık *hastaluhk*
to imagine hayal etmek *hayal etmek*
imagination hayal gücü *hayal gewjew*
important önemli *önemli*
impossible imkansız *imkansuhz*
in -de/-da/-te/-ta *-de/-da/-te/-ta*
in a hurry acelesi olmak *ajelesi olmak*
　》 I am in a hurry acelem var *ajelem var*
in front of önünde *önewnde*
in order to - mek/-mak için *- mek/-mak ichin*
included dahil *da:hil*
independent bağımsız *ba:uhmsuhz*

indigestion hazımsızlık *hazuhmsuhzluhk*
industry sanayi *sanayi*
infection enfeksiyon *enfeksiyon*
infectious bulaşıcı *bulashuhjuh*
inflamed iltihaplı *iltihapluh*
inflammation iltihap *iltihap*
inflatable şişirilebilir *shishirilebilir*
influenza grip *grip*
informal gayriresmi *gayriresmi*
information bilgi *bilgi*
information desk/office danışma
   danuhshma
injection iğne *i:ne*
to injure yaralamak *yaralamak*
   injured yaralı *yaraluh*
   injury yara *yara*
   innocent suçsuz *suchsuz*
   insect böcek *böjek*
   insect bite böcek ısırığı *böjek uhsuhruh:uh*
   insect repellent böcek kovucu *böjek*
      kovuju
   inside içinde, içeride *ichinde, icheride*
   instead of yerine *yerine*
   instructor öğretmen *ö:retmen*
   insulin insülin *insewlin*
   insult hakaret *haka:ret*
   insurance sigorta *sigorta*
to insure sigortalamak *sigortalamak*
   insured sigortalı *sigortaluh*
   intelligent akıllı *akuhlluh*
   interest (money) faiz *faiz*
   interested: to be interested ilgilenmek
      ilgilenmek
   interesting ilginç *ilginch*
   internet internet *internet*
   internet café internet kafé *internet kafé*
   internet connection internet bağlantısı
      internet ba:lantuhsuh
to interpret çevirmek *chevirmek*
   interpreter çevirmen *chevirmen*
   interval (theatre etc.) ara *ara*
   interview görüşme *görewshme*
to introduce tanıştırmak *tanuhshtuhrmak*
   invitation davet *da:vet*

to invite davet etmek *da:vet etmek*
   Ireland İrlanda *irlanda*
   Irish İrlandalı *irlandaluh*
   iron (metal) demir *demir* (for clothes)
      ütü *ewtew*
to iron ütülemek *ewtewlemek*
   is there...? ...var mı? *...var muh*
   Islam islam *islam*
   Islamic islami *isla:mi*
   island ada *ada*
   it o, onu *o, onu*
   itch kaşıntı *kashuhntuh*

J

   jacket ceket *jeket*
   jam reçel *rechel*
   jar kavanoz *kavanoz*
   jazz caz *jaz*
   jeans kot pantolon *kot pantolon*
   jellyfish denizanası *denizanasuh*
   jetty dalgakıran *dalgakuhran*
   jewellery mücevher *mewjevher*
   jeweller's kuyumcu *kuyumju*
   Jewish yahudi *yahudi*
   job iş *ish*
   jogging koşu *koshu*
   joke şaka *shaka*
   journalist gazeteci *gazeteji*
   journey yolculuk *yoljuluk*
   judge hakim *ha:kim*
   jug sürahi *sewra:hi*
   juice su *su*
to jump atlamak *atlamak*
   jumper kazak *kazak*
   junction kavşak *kavshak*
   just (only) sadece *sadeje*

K

to keep saklamak *saklamak*
   keep to the right sağdan gidiniz *sa:*
      dan gidiniz
   kettle çaydanlık *chaydanluhk*
   key anahtar *anahtar*
   key ring anahtarlık *anahtarluhk*

to key in one's PIN number şifre girmek *shifre girmek*

kidney böbrek *böbrek*

to kill öldürmek *öldewrmek*

kilo(gram) kilo(gram) *kilo(gram)*

kilometre kilometre *kilometre*

kind *(sort)* çeşit *cheshit (generous)* nazik *nazik*

king kral *kral*

kiss öpücük *öpewjew*

to kiss öpmek *öpmek*

kitchen mutfak *mutfak*

knickers don *don*

knife bıçak *buhchak*

to knock vurmak *vurmak*

knot düğüm *dew:ewm*

to know *(someone)* tanımak *tanuhmak* *(something)* bilmek *bilmek*

>> I don't know bilmiyorum *bilmiyorum*

L

label etiket *etiket*

lace dantel *dantel*

ladder merdiven *merdiven*

lady hanım *hanuhm*

ladies bayanlar *bayanlar*

lager hafif bira *hafif bira*

lake göl *göl*

lamb *(meat)* kuzu *kuzu*

lamp lamba *lamba*

lamp post sokak lambası *sokak lambasuh*

land toprak *toprak*

to land yere inmek *yere inmek*

landing *(ship etc.)* karaya çıkma *karaya chuhkma*

landlady evsahibesi *evsa:hibesi*

landlord evsahibi *evsa:hibi*

language dil *dil*

laptop dizüstü (bilgisayar) *dizewstew (bilgisayar)*

large büyük *bewyewk*

last son *son*

to last sürmek *sewrmek*

late geç *gech*

later daha sonra *daha sonra*

laugh gülmek *gewlmek*

laundry çamaşır *chamashuhr*

law kanun *ka:nun*

lawyer avukat *avukat*

lazy tembel *tembel*

lead-free kurşunsuz *kurshunsuz*

leaf yaprak *yaprak*

leaflet broşür *broshewr*

to lean out dayanmak *dayanmak*

to learn öğrenmek *ö:renmek*

least: at least en az *en az*

leather deri *deri*

leather goods deri eşya *deri eshya*

to leave *(go away)* ayrılmak *ayruhlmak* *(forget sthg.)* unutmak *unutmak*

lecture ders, konferans *ders, konferans*

left sol *sol*

left luggage office emanet *ema:net*

legal kanuni *kanu:ni*

leisure boş vakit *bosh vakit*

lemon limon *limon*

to lend ödünç vermek *ödewnch vermek*

length uzunluk *uzunluk*

lens *(camera)* mercek *merjek* *(contact)* lens *lens*

lentil mercimek *merjimek*

lesbian lezbiyen *lezbiyen*

less daha az *daha az*

lesson ders *ders*

to let *(allow)* izin vermek *izin vermek* *(rent)* kiraya vermek *kiraya vermek*

letter *(to someone)* mektup *mektup (of alphabet)* harf *harf*

letterbox mektup kutusu *mektup kutusu*

level *(height, standard)* derece *dereje (flat)* düz *dewz*

level crossing tren geçidi *tren gechidi*

library kütüphane *kewtewpha:ne*

licence *(driving)* ehliyet *ehliyet (fishing etc.)* izin *izin*

lid kapak *kapak*

to lie down uzanmak *uzanmak*

life hayat *hayat*

lifeboat cankurtaran botu *jankurtaran botu*

lifeguard cankurtaran *jankurtaran*

lifejacket can yeleği *jan yele:i*

lift asansör *asansör*

to lift kaldırmak *kalduhrmak*

light *(car)* ışık *uhshuhk*

(house) lamba *lamba*

light bulb ampul *ampul*

light *(colour)* açık *achuhk*

(weight) hafif *hafif*

to light yakmak *yakmak*

lighter çakmak *chakmak*

lighter fuel çakmak gazı *chakmak gazuh*

lightning aydınlatma, şimşek *ayduhnlatma, shimshek*

to like hoşlanmak *hoshlanmak*

limited sınırlı *suhnuhrluh*

line hat *hat*

lip dudak *dudak*

lipstick ruj *ruzh*

liqueur likör *likör*

liquid sıvı *suhvuh*

list liste *liste*

to listen *(to)* dinlemek *dinlemek*

litre litre *litre*

litter çöp *chöp*

little çok az *chok az*

 » **a little** biraz *biraz*

to live yaşamak *yashamak*

liver karaciğer *karaji:er*

loan borç *borch*

local yerli *yerli*

lock kilit *kilit*

locker kilitli dolap *kilitli dolap*

lonely yalnız *yalnuhz*

long uzun *uzun*

 » **(a) long time** uzun vakit *uzun vakit*

long-distance call uzak arama *uzak arama*

to look *(at)* bakmak *bakmak*

to look for aramak *aramak*

loose gevşek *gevshek*

lorry kamyon *kamyon*

to lose kaybetmek *kaybetmek*

lost kayıp *kayuhp*

lost property office kayıp eşya bürosu *kayuhp eshya bewrosu*

a lot (of) çok *chok*

lotion losyon *losyon*

lottery piyango *piyango*

loud yüksek sesli *yewksek sesli*

lounge salon *salon*

to love sevmek *sevmek*

low alçak *alchak*

low-fat az yağlı *az ya:luh*

lower daha düşük *daha dewshewk*

lucky: to be lucky şanslı olmak *shansluh: shansluh olmak*

luggage bagaj *bagaj*

lunch öğle yemeği *ö:le yeme:i*

M

machine makina *makina*

mad deli *deli*

magazine mecmua *mejmua*

mail posta *posta*

main asıl *asuhl*

main station ana istasyon *ana istasyon*

to make yapmak *yapmak*

make-up makyaj *makyazh*

male erkek *erkek*

man adam *adam*

manager müdür *mewdewr*

managing director genel müdür *genel mewdewr*

many çok *chok*

 » **not many** az *az*

map harita *harita*

marble mermer *mermer*

market pazar *pazar*

marmalade marmelat *marmelat*

married evli *evli*

 » **to get married** evlenmek *evlenmek*

mascara rimel *rimel*

mask *(diving)* maske *maske*

match *(game)* maç *mach*

material materyal *materyal*

mathematics matematik *matematik*

matter: it doesn't matter sorun: sorun
değil *sorun: sorun de:il*

» what's the matter? sorun nedir?
sorun nedir

mattress yatak *yatak*

mature olgun *olgun*

me beni *beni*

meal yemek *yemek*

mean: what does this mean? anlam ...
ne demek? *anlam ... ne demek?*

meanwhile bu sırada *bu suhrada*

measles kızamık *kuhzamuhk*

» German measles kızamıkçık
kuhzamuhkchuhk

to measure ölçmek *ölchmek*

measurement ölçü *ölchew*

meat et *et*

mechanic tamirci *tamirji*

medical tıbbi *tuhbbi*

medicine (drug) ilaç *ilach* (subject) tıp
tuhp

medieval ortaçağa ait *ortacha:a ait*

Mediterranean Akdeniz *akdeniz*

medium orta *orta*

meeting toplantı *toplantuh*

melon kavun *kavun*

member üye *ewye*

memory hafıza *hafuhza*

memory card hafıza kartı *hafuhza kartuh*

men erkek *erkek*

to mend tamir etmek *tamir etmek*

menu mönü *mönew*

message mesaj *mesazh*

metal metal *metal*

meter sayaç *sayach*

metre metre *metre*

microwave oven mikrodalga fırın
mikrodalga fuhruhn

midday öğle *ö:le*

middle orta *orta*

middle-aged orta yaşlı *orta yashluh*

midnight gece yarısı *geje yaruhsuh*

migraine migren *migren*

mile mil *mil*

milk süt *sewt*

milkshake milkşeyk *milksheyk*

mind: do you mind if...? .... sakıncası
var mı? *....sakuhnjasuh varmuh*

» I don't mind farketmez *farketmez*

mine (of me) benim, benimki *benim,
benimki*

minibar minibar *minibar*

minibus minibüs *minibews*

minute (time) dakika *dakika*

mirror ayna *ayna*

miscarriage düşük *dewshewk*

to miss (bus etc.) kaçırmak *kachuhrmak*
(nostalgia) özlemek *özlemek*

mist sis, duman *sis, duman*

mistake hata *hata*

» to make a mistake hata yapmak *hata
yapmak*

mobile phone cep telefonu *jep telefonu*

model model *model*

modem modem *modem*

modern modern *modern*

moisturiser nemlendirici *nemlendiriji*

moment an, dakika *an dakika*

money para *para*

month ay *ay*

monthly aylık *ayluhk*

monument yapıt *yapuht*

moon ay *ay*

moped moped *moped*

more daha *daha*

morning sabah *sabah*

mortgage ipotek *ipotek*

mosque cami *ja:mi*

mosquito sivrisinek *sivrisinek*

most (of) çoğu *cho:u*

mother anne *anne*

mother-in-law kayınvalide *kayuhnvalide*

motor motor *motor*

motorbike motosiklet *motosiklet*

motorboat motor *motor*

motorway otoyol *otoyol*

mountain dağ *da:*

mountaineering dağcılık *da:juhluhk*
to move hareket etmek *hareket etmek*
to move house taşınmak *tashuhnmak*
MP3-player mp3-çalar *mp üç-chalar*
Mr bay *bay*
Mrs bayan *bayan*
much çok *chok*
» **not much** az *az*
mug (cup) kulplu bardak, kupa *kulplu bardak, kupa*
to mug (someone) (saldırıp) soymak *(salduhruhp) soymak*
museum müze *mewze*
music müzik *mewzik*
musical müzikal *mewzikal*
musician müzisyen *mewzisyen*
Muslim müslüman *mewslewman*
my benim *benim*
mystery gizem *gizem*

N

nail tırnak *tuhrnak*
» **nail clippers/scissors** tırnak makası *tuhrnak makasuh*
» **nail file** tırnak törpüsü *tuhrnak törpewsew*
nail polish tırnak cilası, oje *tuhrnak jilasuh ozhe*
nail polish remover aseton *aseton*
naked çıplak *chuhplak*
name ad *ad*
» **my name is...** adım... *aduhm...*
» **what is your name?** adınız nedir? *aduhnuhz nedir*
napkin peçete *pechete*
nappy bebek bezi *bebek bezi*
national ulusal *ulusal*
nationality uyruk *uyruk*
naughty yaramaz *yaramaz*
nausea mide bulantısı *mi:de bulantuhsuh*
navy deniz kuvvetleri *deniz kuvvetleri*
navy blue lacivert *lajivert*
near yakın *yakuhn*
nearby yakınlarda *yakuhnlarda*

nearest en yakın *en yakuhn*
nearly hemen hemen *hemen hemen*
necessary gerekli, lazım *gerekli la:zuhm*
necklace kolye *kolye*
nectarine nektarin *nektarin*
needle iğne *i:ne*
negative (photo) negatif *negatif*
neighbour komşu *komshu*
neither... nor... ne... ne... *ne... ne...*
nephew yeğen *ye:en*
never asla *asla*
new yeni *yeni*
New Year's Day yılbaşı *yuhlbashuh*
news haberler *haberler*
newspaper gazete *gazete*
next to yanında *yanuhnda*
nice güzel *gewzel*
niece yeğen *ye:en*
night gece *geje*
nightclub gece kulübü *geje kulewbew*
no hayır *ha:yuhr*
no longer/no more artık *artuhk*
nobody hiç kimse *hich kimse*
noise gürültü *gewrewltew*
noisy gürültülü *gewrewltewlew*
non-alcoholic alkolsüz *alkolsewz*
none hiçbir *hichbir*
non-smoking sigara içilmez *sigara ichilmez*
normal normal *normal*
normally normalde *normalde*
north kuzey *kuzey*
nosebleed burun kanaması *burun kanamasuh*
not değil *de:il*
note (bank) kağıt para *ka:uht para*
nothing hiç bir şey *hich bir shey*
» **nothing else** başka hiç bir şey *bashka hich bir shey*
now şimdi *shimdi*
nowhere hiç bir yerde *hich bir yerde*
nuclear power nükleer güç *newkleer gewch*
number sayı, rakam, numara *sayuh,*

rakam, numara
nurse hemşire *hemshire*
nut fındık fıstık gibi sert kabuklu yemiş *fuhnduhk fuhstuhk gibi sert kabuklu yemish*

O

oar kürek *kewrek*
occasionally bazen *ba:zen*
occupied *(seat)* dolu *dolu*
odd *(not even)* tek *tek*
of course tabii *tabii*
off *(tv, light)* kapalı *kapaluh*
(milk) bozuk *bozuk*
offended: to be offended gücenmek *gewjenmek*
offer teklif *teklif*
» special offer özel fiyat *özel fiyat*
office ofis, büro *ofis, bewro*
official resmi *resmi*
often sık sık *suhk suhk*
» how often? ne sıklıkta *ne suhkluhkta*
oil yağ *ya:*
OK tamam *tamam*
old *(opp. of new)* eski *eski (opp. of young)* yaşlı *yashluh*
old-fashioned eski moda *eski moda*
olive zeytin *zeytin*
» olive oil zeytin yağı *zeytin ya:uh*
once bir defa *bir defa*
one bir *bir*
one-way street tek-yön yol *tek-yön yol*
onion soğan *so:an*
only yalnız *yalnuhz*
open açık *achuhk*
to open açmak *achmak*
opera opera *opera*
operation ameliyat *ameliyat*
opinion görüş *görewsh*
» in my opinion bence *benje*
opposite *(contrary)* zıt *zuht*
optician gözlükçü *gözlewkchew*
or veya *veya*
orange *(fruit)* portakal *portakal (colour)*

turuncu *turunju*
orchestra orkestra *orkestra*
to order ısmarlamak *uhsmarlamak*
ordinary sıradan *suhradan*
organic food organik gıda *organik guhda*
to organise düzenlemek *dewzenlemek*
other başka *bashka*
others başkaları *bashkalaruh*
our bizim *bizim*
ours bizim, bizimki *bizim, bizimki*
outdoor/outside dışarı *duhsharuh*
outdoors dışarıda *duhsharuhda*
over üstünde *ewstewnde*
owner sahip *sahip*
ozone-friendly ozon-dostu *ozon-dostu*
ozone layer ozon tabakası *ozon tabakasuh*

P

pacemaker kalp pili *kalp pili*
package tour tur *tur*
packet paket *paket*
padlock asma kilit *asma kilit*
page sayfa *sayfa*
pain ağrı *a:ruh*
painful ağrılı *a:ruhluh*
painkiller ağrı kesici *a:ruh kesiji*
to paint *(picture)* resmini yapmak *resmini yapmak*
painter ressam *ressam*
painting resim *resim*
pair çift *chift*
palace saray *saray*
pale solgun *solgun*
pants don *don*
paper kağıt *ka:uht*
paralysed felçli *felchli*
parcel paket *paket*
pardon? efendim? *efendim*
parents anne baba *anne baba*
park park *park*
to park park etmek *park etmek*
parking park etme *park etme*
parking meter otopark sayacı *otopark*

sayajuh

parliament parlamento *parlamento*

part parça *parcha*

particular: in particular özel: özellikle *özel: özellikle*

partly kısmen *kuhsmen*

partner ortak *ortak*

party *(political)* parti *parti*

to pass *(on road)* geçmek *gechmek*
(salt etc.) vermek *vermek (exam, test)*
geçmek *gechmek*

passenger yolcu *yolju*

passport pasaport *pasaport*

passport control pasaport kontrol *pasaport kontrol*

past geçmiş *gechmish*
 ›› in the past geçmişte *gechmishte*

pasta makarna *makarna*

pastry hamur *hamur*

path yol *yol*

patient *(adj.)* sabırlı *sabuhrluh (hospital)* hasta *hasta*

pattern desen *desen*

pavement kaldırım *kalduhruhm*

to pay ödemek *ödemek*

peach şeftali *shefta:li*

peanuts yer fıstığı *yer fuhstuh:uh*

pedal pedal *pedal*

pedestrian yaya *yaya*

pedestrian crossing yaya geçidi *yaya gechidi*

peg mandal *mandal*

pen dolma kalem *dolma kalem*

pencil kurşun kalem *kurshun kalem*

penfriend mektup arkadaşı *mektup arkadashuh*

penicillin penisilin *penisilin*

pension emekli maaşı *emekli maashuh*

pensioner emekli *emekli*

people insanlar *insanlar*

peppermint nane *na:ne*

per her *her*

perfect mükemmel *mewkemmel*

performance gösteri *gösteri*

perfume parfüm *parfewm*

perhaps belki *belki*

period *(menstrual)* adet *a:det*
 ›› period pains adet ağrısı *a:det a:ruhsuh*

perm perma *perma*

permit izin *izin*

to permit izin vermek *izin vermek*

person kişi *kishi*

personal kişisel *kishisel*

petrol benzin *benzin*

petrol station benzin istasyonu *benzin istasyonu*

phone card telefon kartı *telefon kartuh*

photocopy fotokopi *fotokopi*

photo fotoğraf *foto:raf*

photographer fotoğrafçı *foto:rafchuh*

phrase book pratik konuşma rehberi *pratik konushma rehberi*

piano piyano *piyano*

to pick *(choose)* seçmek *sechmek*
(flowers etc.) toplamak *toplamak*

to pick up almak *almak*

picnic piknik *piknik*

picture resim *resim*

piece parça *parcha*

pier iskele *iskele*

pig domuz *domuz*

pill hap *hap*

pillow yastık *yastuhk*

pillowcase yastık kılıfı *yastuhk kuhluhfuh*

pilot pilot *pilot*

pin toplu iğne *toplu i:ne*

pink pembe *pembe*

pipe *(drain)* boru *boru (smoking)* pipo *pipo*

pitch *(on campsite)* saha *sa:ha*

place *(seat)* yer *yer*

plain düz, sade *dewz, sa:de*

plane uçak *uchak*

plank uzun tahta *uzun tahta*

plant bitki *bitki*

plaster plaster *plaster*

plastic plastik *plastik*

plastic bag naylon poşet *naylon poshet*

plate tabak *tabak*

platform peron *peron*

play *(theatre)* oyun *oyun*

to play oynamak *oynamak*

please lütfen *lewtfen*

pleased memnun *memnun*

>> pleased to meet you memnun oldum
memnun oldum

plenty *(of)* çok *chok*

pliers kerpeten *kerpeten*

plug *(bath)* tıpa *tuhpa (electrical)* fiş *fish*

plumber su tesisatçısı *su tesisatchuhsuh*

pneumonia zatürre *zatewrre*

pocket cep *jep*

point nokta *nokta*

poison zehir *zehir*

poisonous zehirli *zehirli*

police polis *polis*

police car polis arabası *polis arabasuh*

police station polis karakolu *polis
karakolu*

polish cila *jila*

polite kibar *kibar*

politician politikacı *politikajuh*

political politik *politik*

politics politika *politika*

polluted kirli *kirli*

pollution kirlilik *kirlilik*

pool *(swimming)* havuz *havuz*

poor fakir *fakir*

pop music pop müziği *pop mewzi:i*

Pope Papa *papa*

pork domuz eti *domuz eti*

port *(harbour)* liman *liman (wine)* porto
(şarabı) *porto (sharabuh)*

portable portatif *portatif*

portion porsiyon *porsiyon*

portrait portre *portre*

positive pozitif *pozitif*

possible mümkün *mewmkewn*

possibly olabilir *olabilir*

post posta *posta*

to post postalamak *postalamak*

postbox posta kutusu *posta kutusu*

postcard kartpostal *kartpostal*

postcode posta kodu *posta kodu*

poster poster *poster*

postman postacı *postajuh*

post office postane *posta:ne*

to postpone ertelemek *ertelemek*

pot tencere *tenjere*

pottery seramik *seramik*

potty *(child's)* lazımlık *la:zuhmluhk*

pound *(sterling)* sterlin *sterlin*

to pour dökmek *dökmek*

powder pudra *pudra*

power *(electricity)* elektrik *elektrik
(strength)* güç *gewch*

power cut elektrik kesintisi *elektrik
kesintisi*

pram çocuk arabası *chojuk arabasuh*

to prefer tercih etmek *terjih etmek*

pregnant hamile *ha:mile*

prescription reçete *rechete*

present *(gift)* hediye *hediye*

press *(newspapers)* basın *basuhn*

to press basmak *basmak*

pressure baskı *baskuh*

pretty güzel *gewzel*

price fiyat *fiyat*

priest papaz *papaz*

prime minister başbakan *bashbakan*

prince prens *prens*

princess prenses *prenses*

print *(photo)* baskı *baskuh*

to print basmak *basmak*

prison hapishane *hapisha:ne*

private özel *özel*

prize ödül *ödewl*

probably herhalde *herhalde*

problem problem *problem*

product ürün *ewrewn*

profession meslek *meslek*

professor profesör *profesör*

profit kar *kar*

programme program *program*

prohibited yasak *yasak*

to promise söz vermek *söz vermek*

to pronounce telaffuz etmek *telaffuz etmek*

properly doğru *do:ru*
property mülk *mewlk*
protestant protestan *protestan*
public halk *halk*
public holiday resmi tatil *resmi ta:til*
to **pull** çekmek *chekmek*
to **pump up** şişirmek *shishirmek*
puncture lastik patlaması *lastik patlamasuh*
pure öz *öz*
purple mor *mor*
purse cüzdan *jewzdan*
to **push** itmek *itmek*
push-chair puset *puset*
to **put down** koymak *koymak*
to **put on** (clothes) giymek *giymek*
pyjamas pijama *pizhama*

Q

quality kalite *kalite*
quarter çeyrek *cheyrek*
quay rıhtım *ruhhtuhm*
queen kraliçe *kraliche*
question soru *soru*
queue sıra *suhra*
quick(ly) çabuk *chabuk*
quiet sessiz *sessiz*
quite oldukça *oldukcha*

R

rabbi haham *haham*
rabbit tavşan *tavshan*
rabies kuduz *kuduz*
racecourse pist *pist*
racing yarış *yaruhsh*
racket raket *raket*
radiator kalorifer *kalorifer*
radio radyo *radyo*
railway demiryolu *demiryolu*
railway station istasyon *istasyon*
rain yağmur *ya:mur*
» **it's raining** yağmur yağıyor *ya:mur ya:uhyor*
raincoat yağmurluk *ya:murluk*

ramp rampa *rampa*
to **rape** tecavüz etmek *tejavewz etmek*
rare (steak) az pişmiş *az pishmish*
rash döküntü *dökewntew*
rate (ratio) oran *oran* (tariff) fiyat *fiyat*
rather (quite) oldukça *oldukcha*
raw çiğ *chi:*
razor tıraş makinesi *tuhrash makinesi*
razor blade jilet *zhilet*
to **reach** ulaşmak *ulashmak*
to **read** okumak *okumak*
reading okuma *okuma*
ready hazır *hazuhr*
real (authentic) gerçek *gerchek*
really gerçekten *gerchekten*
reason sebep *sebep*
receipt fatura *fatura*
reception resepsiyon *resepsiyon*
receptionist resepsiyon memuru *resepsiyon memuru*
recipe yemek tarifi *yemek ta:rifi*
to **recognise** tanımak *tanuhmak*
to **recommend** tavsiye etmek *tavsiye etmek*
record kayıt *kayuht*
to **record** kayıt etmek *kayuht etmek*
to **recover** iyileşmek *iyileshmek*
red kırmızı *kuhrmuhzuh*
to **refill** yeniden doldurmak *yeniden doldurmak*
refrigerator buzdolabı *buzdolabuh*
refugee mülteci *mewlteji*
refund para iadesi *para iadesi*
region bölge *bölge*
regional bölgesel *bölgesel*
registration (car) plaka numarası *plaka numarasuh*
religion din *din*
to **remain** kalmak *kalmak*
to **remember** hatırlamak *hatuhrlamak*
to **remove** kaldırmak *kalduhrmak* (tooth) çekmek *chekmek*
rent kira *kira*
to **rent** kiralamak *kiralamak*
to **repair** tamir etmek *ta:mir etmek*

to repeat tekrar etmek *tekrar etmek*
   report rapor *rapor*
to rescue kurtarmak *kurtarmak*
   reservation rezervasyon *rezervasyon*
to reserve ayırmak *ayuhrmak*
   reserved ayrılmış *ayruhlmuhsh*
to rest dinlenmek *dinlenmek*
   restaurant restoran *restoran*
   result sonuç *sonuch*
   retired emekli *emekli*
   return (ticket) gidiş-dönüş *gidish-dönewsh*
to return geri dönmek *geri dönmek*
to reverse (car) geri gitmek *geri gitmek*
   reverse-charge call ödemeli telefon *ödemeli telefon*
   rice pirinç *pirinch* (cooked) pilav *pilav*
   rich zengin *zengin*
to ride (bike, horse) binmek *binmek*
   right sağ *sa:* (correct) doğru *do:ru*
   ›› to be right haklı olmak *hakluh olmak*
   ›› you're right haklısınız *hakluhsuhnuhz*
   right-hand side sağ tarafta *sa: tarafta*
   ring (jewellery) yüzük *yewzewk*
   river nehir *nehir*
   road yol *yol*
   roadworks yol tamiratı *yol ta:mira:tuh*
   roast fırında kızarmış *fuhruhnda kuhzarmuhsh*
to rob soymak *soymak*
   robbery soygun *soygun*
   rock climbing kaya tırmanışı *kaya tuhrmanuhshuh*
   roof çatı *chatuh*
   room oda *oda*
   room service oda servisi *oda servisi*
   rope halat *halat*
   rose gül *gewl*
   rotten çürük *chewrewk*
   rough (sea) dalgalı *dalgaluh* (surface) sert *sert*
   round yuvarlak *yuvarlak*
   roundabout göbek *göbek*
   row (theatre) sıra *suhra*

   royal kraliyet *kraliyet*
   rubbish çöp *chöp*
   rucksack sırt çantası *suhrt chantasuh*
   rude kaba *kaba*
   ruins harabeler *harabeler*
to run koşmak *koshmak*
   rush hour kalabalık saat *kalabaluhk saat*
   rusty paslı *pasluh*

S

   sad üzgün *ewzgewn*
   safe (strongbox) güvenli *gewvenli*
   safety pin çengelli iğne *chengelli i:ne*
   sail yelken *yelken*
   sailing yelken sporu *yelken sporu*
   sailing boat yelkenli *yelkenli*
   sailor denizci *denizji*
   saint aziz *aziz*
   salad salata *salata*
   sale (reduced prices) ucuzluk *ujuzluk*
   salmon som balığı *som baluh:uh*
   salt tuz *tuz*
   salty tuzlu *tuzlu*
   same aynı *aynuh*
   sample örnek *örnek*
   sand kum *kum*
   sandals sandalet *sandalet*
   sandwich sandviç *sandvich*
   sanitary towel hijyenik kadın bağı *hizhyenik kaduhn ba:uh*
   satisfied memnun *memnun*
   sauce sos *sos*
   saucepan tencere *tenjere*
   saucer fincan tabağı *finjan taba:uh*
   sauna sauna *sauna*
   sausage sosis *sosis*
to save (money) biriktirmek *biriktirmek*
to say söylemek *söylemek*
to scald haşlamak *hashlamak*
   scales tartı *tartuh*
   scarf eşarp *esharp*
   scenery manzara *manzara*
   school okul *okul*
   science bilim *bilim*

scientist bilim adamı *bilim adamuh*

scissors makas *makas*

scooter skuter *skuter*

score: what's the score? sonuç: sonuç ne? *sonuch: sonuch ne*

Scotland İskoçya *iskochya*

Scottish İskoçyalı *iskochyaluh*

to scratch çizmek *chizmek*

screen ekran *ekran*

screw vida *vida*

screwdriver tornavida *tornavida*

scuba diving aletli dalış *aletli daluhsh*

sculpture heykel *heykel*

sea deniz *deniz*

seafood deniz mahsulleri *deniz mahsulleri*

seasickness deniz tutması *deniz tutmasuh*

season mevsim *mevsim*

seat yer *yer*

seatbelt kemer *kemer*

second ikinci *ikinji*

secret sır *suhr*

secretary sekreter *sekreter*

section bölüm *bölewm*

to see görmek *görmek*

self-catering (yemeksiz) sadece konaklama *(yemeksiz) sadeje konaklama*

to sell satmak *satmak*

to send göndermek *göndermek*

senior citizen yaşlı vatandaş *yashluh vatandash*

sensible hassas, akla yatkın *hassas akla yatkuhn*

sentence cümle *jewmle (legal)* ceza *jeza*

separate(d) ayrı *ayruh*

serious ciddi *jiddi (grave)* vahim *vahim (important)* önemli *önemli*

to serve hizmet etmek *hizmet etmek*

service (charge) servis (ücreti) *servis (ewjreti) (church)* ibadet *iba:det*

several birkaç *birkach*

to sew dikmek *dikmek*

sewing dikiş *dikish*

sex (gender) cinsiyet *jinsiyet (intercourse)*

cinsel ilişki *jinsel ilishki*

shade (not sunny) gölge *gölge*

shadow gölge *gölge*

shampoo şampuan *shampuan*

sharp keskin *keskin*

shave traş *trash*

to shave traş olmak *trash olmak*

shaving cream/foam traş kremi/köpüğü *trash kremi/köpew:ew*

she o *o*

sheep koyun *koyun*

sheet (for bed) çarşaf *charshaf (paper)* kağıt *ka:uht*

shelf raf *raf*

shell kabuk *kabuk*

shellfish kabuklu deniz hayvanı *kabuklu deniz hayvanuh*

shiny parlak *parlak*

ship gemi *gemi*

shirt gömlek *gömlek*

shock şok *shok*

shoe(s) ayakkabı *ayakkabuh*

shoe polish ayakkabı boyası *ayakkabuh boyasuh*

shoe repairer's ayakkabı tamircisi *ayakkabuh tamirjisi*

shoe shop ayakkabıcı *ayakkabuhjuh*

shoe size ayak numarası *ayak numarasuh*

shop dükkan *dewkkan*

shopping centre alışveriş merkezi *aluhshverish merkezi*

short kısa *kuhsa*

shorts şort *short*

shoulder omuz *omuz*

to show göstermek *göstermek*

shower duş *dush*

shut kapalı *kapaluh*

shutter kepenk *kepenk*

sick hasta *hasta*

» to be sick kusmak *kusmak*

» I feel sick midem bulanıyor *mi:dem bulanuhyor*

sick bag kusma torbası *kusma torbasuh*

side kenar *kenar*

sight *(vision)* görüş *görewsh* (tourists) görülecek yer *görewlejek yer*
sightseeing gezme *gezme*
sign işaret *isha:ret*
to sign imza atmak *imza: atmak*
signal sinyal *sinyal*
signature imza *imza:*
silence sessizlik *sessizlik*
silk ipek *ipek*
silver gümüş *gewmewsh*
SIM card SIM kart *Sim kart*
similar benzer *benzer*
simple basit *basit*
since -den/-dan/-ten/-tan beri *-den/-dan/-ten/-tan beri*
to sing şarkı söylemek *sharkuh söylemek*
single *(room)* tek kişilik *tek kishilik* (ticket) gidiş *gidish* (unmarried) bekar *bekar*
sink lavabo *lavabo*
sinus infection sinüzit *sinewzit*
sister kız kardeş *kuhz kardesh*
sister-in-law *(wife's sister)* baldız *balduhz* (husband's sister) görümce *görewmje*
to sit *(down)* oturmak *oturmak*
size *(clothes)* beden *beden* (shoes) numara *numara*
skates *(ice)* paten *paten*
ski kayak *kayak*
to ski kayak yapmak *kayak yapmak*
ski boots kayak ayakkabısı *kayak ayakkabuhsuh*
skiing kayak *kayak*
ski-lift lift *lift*
skimmed milk yağsız süt *ya:suhz sewt*
skin deri *deri*
ski pole kayak sopası *kayak sopasuh*
skirt etek *etek*
ski-run/slope kayak pisti *kayak pisti*
sky gökyüzü *gökyewzew*
to sleep uyumak *uyumak*
sleeper/sleeping-car yataklı vagon *yatakluh vagon*
sleeping bag uyku tulumu *uyku tulumu*
sleeve kol *kol*

slice dilim *dilim*
to slice dilimlemek *dilimlemek*
sliced dilimlenmiş *dilimlenmish*
slim ince *inje*
slippery kaygan *kaygan*
slow(ly) yavaş *yavash*
to slow down yavaşlamak *yavashlamak*
small küçük *kewchewk*
smell koku *koku*
to smell koklamak *koklamak* (of) ima etmek *i:ma: etmek* (bad/good) kokmak *kokmak*
to smile gülümsemek *gewlewmsemek*
smoke duman *duman*
to smoke sigara içmek *sigara ichmek*
smooth engelsiz, kolay *engelsiz, kolay*
to sneeze hapşırmak *hapshuhrmak*
snorkel şnorkel *shnorkel*
snow kar *kar*
to snow kar yağmak *kar ya:mak*
  » it's snowing kar yağıyor *kar ya:uhyor*
snowboarding snowboard *snowboard*
so onun için *onun ichin*
soap sabun *sabun*
sock çorap *chorap*
socket priz *priz*
soda *(water)* soda *soda*
soft yumuşak *yumushak*
soft drink meşrubat, alkolsüz içecek *meshrubat, alkolsewz ichejek*
software bilgisayar programı *bilgisayar programuh*
soldier asker *asker*
sold out kalmadı *kalmaduh*
solicitor avukat *avukat*
some bazı *ba:zuh*
somehow nasılsa *nasuhlsa*
someone birisi *birisi*
something bir şey *bir shey*
sometimes bazen *ba:zen*
somewhere bir yerde *bir yerde*
son oğul *o:ul*
son-in-law damat *da:mat*

soon yakında *yakuhnda*
» as soon as possible en kısa zamanda *en kuhsa zamanda*
sore throat boğaz ağrısı *bo:az a:ruhsuh*
sorry: I'm sorry özür dilerim *özewr dilerim*
to sort ayırmak *ayuhrmak*
sound ses *ses*
sour ekşi *ekshi*
south güney *gewney*
souvenir hediyelik eşya *hediyelik eshya*
to speak konuşmak *konushmak*
special özel *özel*
special offer özel fiyat *özel fiyat*
speciality özellik *özellik*
speed hız *huhz*
speed limit azami hız *a:zami: huhz*
to spend (money) harcamak *harjamak* (time) vakit geçirmek *vakit gechirmek*
spice baharat *baharat*
spicy baharatlı *baharatluh*
spirits alkollü içki *alkollew ichki*
splinter kıymık *kuhymuhk*
to spoil bozmak *bozmak*
spoon kaşık *kashuhk*
sport spor *spor*
to sprain burkmak *burkmak*
sprained burkulmuş *burkulmush*
square (in town) meydan *meydan* (shape) kare *kare*
stadium stadyum *stadyum*
stain leke *leke*
stairs merdiven *merdiven*
stalls (theatre) koltuk *koltuk*
stamp (postage) pul *pul*
to stand ayakta durmak *ayakta durmak*
start başlangıç *bashlanguhch*
starter (food) meze *meze*
station istasyon *istasyon*
stationer's kırtasiyeci *kuhrtasiyeji*
statue heykel *heykel*
to stay (live) yaşamak *yashamak* (remain) kalmak *kalmak*
to steal çalmak *chalmak*

steamed buğulanmış *bu:ulanmuhsh*
steel çelik *chelik*
steep dik *dik*
step (footstep) adım *aduhm* (stairs) basamak *basamak*
stepbrother üvey erkek kardeş *ewvey erkek kardesh*
stepchildren üvey çocuk *ewvey chojuk*
stepfather üvey baba *ewvey baba*
stepmother üvey anne *ewvey anne*
stepsister üvey kız kardeş *ewvey kuhz kardesh*
steering wheel direksiyon *direksiyon*
stereo stereo *stereo*
sterling: pound sterling sterlin *sterlin*
steward kabin memuru *kabin memuru*
stewardess hostes *hostes*
to stick: it's stuck yapışmak: takıldı *yapuhshmak: takuhlduh*
sticky yapışkan *yapuhshkan*
stiff sert *sert*
still (yet) hala *ha:la:*
still (non-fizzy) köpüksüz *köpewksewz*
sting sokma, iğne *sokma, i:ne*
to sting sokmak *sokmak*
stock cube Et suyu tablet *et suyu tablet*
stock exchange borsa *borsa*
stolen: my … has been stolen … çalındı … *chaluhnduh*
stomach ache mide ağrısı *mi:de a:ruhsuh*
stomach upset mide bozukluğu *mi:de bozuklu:u*
stone taş *tash*
to stop durmak *durmak*
stop! dur! *dur*
stopcock tıpa *tuhpa*
story öykü *öykew*
storey kat *kat*
stove ocak *ojak*
straight düz *dewz*
» straight on doğru *do:ru*
strange garip *garip*
strap bağ *ba:*
straw (drinking) çubuk *chubuk*

strawberries çilek *chilek*

street sokak *sokak*

stretcher sedye *sedye*

strike grev *grev*

» **on strike** grevde *grevde*

string ip *ip*

striped çizgili *chizgili*

strong kuvvetli *kuvvetli*

student öğrenci *ö:renji*

to **study** ders çalışmak *ders chaluhshmak*

stupid aptal *aptal*

style biçim *bichim*

subtitle alt yazı *alt yazuh*

suburb banliyö *banliyö*

to **succeed** başarmak *basharmak*

success başarı *basharuh*

such böyle, gibi *böyle, gibi*

suddenly birdenbire *birdenbire*

sugar şeker *sheker*

suit takım elbise *takuhm elbise*

suitcase bavul *bavul*

sun güneş *gewnesh*

to **sunbathe** güneşlenmek *gewneshlenmek*

sunburn güneş yanığı *gewnesh yanuh:uh*

sunglasses güneş gözlüğü *gewnesh gözlew:ew*

sunny güneşli *gewneshli*

sunstroke güneş çarpması *gewnesh charpmasuh*

suntan bronzlaşma *bronzlashma*

suntan lotion güneş sonrası losyonu *gewnesh sonrasuh losyonu*

supermarket süpermarket *sewpermarket*

supplement ek ücret *ek ewjret*

suppose: I suppose so herhalde *herhalde*

suppository fitil *fitil*

sure emin *emin*

surface yüzey *yewzey*

to **surf** (internet) sörf yapmak *sörf yapmak*

surname soyadı *soyaduh*

surprise sürpriz *sewrpriz*

surprised şaşkın *shashkuhn*

surrounded by çevrili *chevrili*

to **swallow** yutmak *yutmak*

to **sweat** terlemek *terlemek*

sweet tatlı *tatluh*

sweetener tadlandırıcı *tadlanduhruhjuh*

sweets şeker *sheker*

swelling şiş *shish*

to **swim** yüzmek *yewzmek*

swimming pool yüzme havuzu *yewzme havuzu*

swimming trunks mayo *mayo*

swimsuit mayo *mayo*

switch düğme *dew:me*

to **switch off** kapatmak *kapatmak*

to **switch on** açmak *achmak*

swollen şiş *shish*

symptom belirti *belirti*

synagogue sinagog *sinagog*

synthetic sentetik *sentetik*

syrup şurup *shurup*

system sistem *sistem*

T

table masa *masa*

table tennis masa tenisi *masa tenisi*

tablecloth masa örtüsü *masa örtewsew*

tablet hap *hap*

tailor terzi *terzi*

to **take** almak (exam) girmek *girmek* (photo) çekmek *chekmek* (bus) binmek *binmek*

to **take away** alıp götürmek *aluhp götewrmek*

to **take off** (clothes) çıkarmak *chuhkarmak* (plane) kalkmak *kalkmak*

taken (seat) dolu *dolu*

to **talk** konuşmak *konushmak*

tall uzun *uzun*

tampon tampon *tampon*

tap musluk *musluk*

tap water musluk suyu *musluk suyu*

tape (adhesive) bant *bant* (cassette) teyp *teyp*

tape measure şerit metre *sherit metre*

tariff tarife *ta:rife*

taste tat *tat*

to taste tatmak *tatmak*

tax vergi *vergi*

taxi taksi *taksi*

taxi rank taksi durağı *taksi dura:uh*

tea çay *chay*

to teach öğretmek *ö:retmek*

teacher öğretmen *ö:retmen*

team takım *takuhm*

teapot demlik *demlik*

tear *(rip)* yırtık *yuhrtuhk* *(cry)* gözyaşı *gözyashuh*

teaspoon çay kaşığı *chay kashuh:uh*

teat *(for baby's bottle)* biberon emziği *biberon emzi:i*

technical teknik *teknik*

technology teknoloji *teknoloji*

teenager *(female)* gençkız *genchkuhz* *(male)* delikanlı *delikanluh*

telephone telefon *telefon*

telephone box telefon kulübesi *telefon kulewbesi*

telephone card telefon kartı *telefon kartuh*

telephone directory telefon rehberi *telefon rehberi*

to telephone telefon etmek *telefon etmek*

television televizyon *televizyon*

to tell söylemek *söylemek*

temperature ısı *uhsuh*

to have a temperature ateşi ölçmek *ateshi ölchmek*

temporary geçici *gechiji*

tennis tenis *tenis*

tennis court tenis kortu *tenis kortu*

tent çadır *chaduhr*

tent peg çadır çivisi *chaduhr chivisi*

tent pole çadır direği *chaduhr dire:i*

terminal terminal *terminal*

terminus son durak *son durak*

terrace teras *teras*

terrible çok kötü *chok kötew*

terrorist terorist *terorist*

text message yazılı mesaj *yazuhluh mesaj*

thank you *(very much)* (çok) teşekkür ederim *(chok) teshekkewr ederim*

that *(one)* şu (şunu) *shu (shunu)*

theatre tiyatro *tiyatro*

theft hırsızlık *huhrsuhzluhk*

their onların *onlaruhn*

theirs onların, onlarınki *onlaruhn, onlaruhnki*

then sonra *sonra*

there orada *orada*

there is/are ....var ...*var*

there it is işte burada *ishte burada*

therefore onun için *onun ichin*

these bunlar *bunlar*

they onlar *onlar*

thick kalın *kaluhn*

thief hırsız *huhrsuhz*

thin ince *inje*

thing şey *shey*

to think *(believe)* düşünmek *dewshewnmek*

>> **I (don't) think so** bence öyle (değil) *benje öyle (de:il)*

third üçüncü *ewchewnjew*

thirsty susamış *susamuhsh*

this *(one)* bu (bunu) *bu (bunu)*

those şunlar *shunlar*

thread iplik *iplik*

threat tehdit *tehdit*

through boyunca *boyunja*

to throw atmak *atmak*

thunder gök gürültüsü *gök gewrewltewsew*

ticket bilet *bilet*

ticket office bilet gişesi *bilet gishesi*

tide akıntı, gelgit *akuhntuh, gelgit*

tie kravat *kravat*

tight sıkı *suhkuh*

tights külotlu çorap *kewlotlu chorap*

till *(until)* -e/-a/-ye/-ya kadar *-e/-a/-ye/-ya kadar*

time *(once etc.)* kere, defa *kere, defa* *(general)* zaman *zaman*

timetable tarife *ta:rife*

tin *(teneke)* kutu *(teneke) kutu*

tin foil yaldız kağıt *yalduhz ka:uht*

tinned *(food)* konserve *konserve*

tin opener konserve açacağı *konserve achaja:uh*

tip *(in restaurant etc.)* bahşiş *bahshish*

tired yorgun *yorgun*

tissues kağıt mendil *ka:uht mendil*

toast kızarmış ekmek *kuhzarmuhsh ekmek*

tobacco tütün *tewtewn*

today bugün *bugewn*

toilet tuvalet *tuvalet*

toilet paper tuvalet kağıdı *tuvalet ka:uhduh*

toll geçiş ücreti *gechish ewjreti*

tomato domates *domates*

tomorrow yarın *yaruhn*

tongue dil *dil*

tonight bu gece *bu geje*

too *(as well)* de/da/te/ta *de/da/te/ta*

tool alet *a:let*

toolkit alet çantası *a:let chantasuh*

tooth diş *dish*

toothache diş ağrısı *dish a:ruhsuh*

toothbrush diş fırçası *dish fuhrchasuh*

toothpaste diş macunu *dish majunu*

toothpick kürdan *kewrdan*

torch el feneri *el feneri*

torn yırtık *yuhrtuhk*

total toplam *toplam*

totally toplam olarak *toplam olarak*

to touch dokunmak *dokunmak*

tough *(difficult)* zor *zor*

tour tur *tur*

tourism turizm *turizm*

tourist turist *turist*

tourist office turizm bürosu *turizm bewrosu*

tournament turnuva *turnuva*

towards doğru *do:ru*

towel havlu *havlu*

tower kule *kule*

town şehir *shehir*

town centre şehir merkezi *shehir merkezi*

tow rope çekme halatı *chekme halatuh*

toy oyuncak *oyunjak*

track iz *iz*

traditional geleneksel *geleneksel*

traffic trafik *trafik*

traffic jam trafik sıkışıklığı *trafik suhkuhshuhkluh:uh*

traffic lights trafik ışıkları *trafik uhshuhklaruh*

train tren *tren*

 )) by train trenle *trenle*

trainers spor ayyakkabı *spor ayyakkabuh*

tram tramvay *tramvay*

tranquilliser sakinleştirici *sakinleshtiriji*

to translate çevirmek *chevirmek*

translation çeviri *cheviri*

to travel seyahat etmek *seyahat etmek*

travel agency seyahat acentası *seyahat ajentasuh*

traveller's cheque seyahat çeki *seyahat cheki*

travel sickness araç tutması *arach tutmasuh*

treatment tedavi *teda:vi*

tree ağaç *a:ach*

trip yolculuk *yoljuluk*

trousers pantolon *pantolon*

true: that's true doğru *do:ru*

to try denemek *denemek*

to try on denemek *denemek*

T-shirt tişört *tishört*

tube *(pipe)* tüp *tewp* (underground) metro *metro*

tuna tuna balığı *tuna baluh:uh*

tunnel tünel *tewnel*

turn: it's my turn sıra: benim sıram *suhra: benim suhram*

to turn dönmek *dönmek*

to turn off kapatmak *kapatmak*

turning dönemeç *dönemech*

twice iki kez *iki kez*

twin beds çift yatak *chift yatak*

twins ikizler *ikizler*

twisted burkulmuş *burkulmush*

type *(sort)* çeşit *cheshit*

to type daktilo etmek *daktilo etmek*
  typical tipik *tipik*

U

USB lead USB girişi *usb girishi*
ugly çirkin *chirkin*
ulcer ülser *ewlser*
umbrella şemsiye *shemsiye*
uncle *(father's brother)* amca *amja*
  (mother's brother) dayı *dayuh*
uncomfortable rahatsız *rahatsuhz*
under altında *altuhnda*
underground metro *metro*
underpants külot *kewlot*
underpass alt geçit *alt gechit*
to understand anlamak *anlamak*
underwater sualtı *sualtuh*
underwear iç çamaşırı *ich chamashuhruh*
to undress soyunmak *soyunmak*
unemployed işsiz *ishsiz*
unemployment işsizlik *ishsizlik*
unfortunately maalesef *maalesef*
unhappy mutsuz *mutsuz*
uniform üniforma *ewniforma*
university üniversite *ewniversite*
unleaded petrol kurşunsuz benzin *kurshunsuz benzin*
unlimited sınırsız *suhnuhrsuhz*
unpleasant hoş olmayan *hosh olmayan*
to unscrew vidayı çıkarmak *vidayuh chuhkarmak*
until -e/-a/-ye/-ya kadar *-e/-a/-ye/-ya kadar*
unusual az görülen *az görewlen*
unwell hasta *hasta*
up üst *ewst*
up the road yolun yukarısında *yolun yukaruhsuhnda*
upper üst *ewst*
upstairs üst kat *ewst kat*
urgent acele *ajele*
urine idrar *idrar*
us bizi *bizi*
to use kullanmak *kullanmak*

useful yararlı *yararluh*
useless yararsız *yararsuhz*
usually genellikle *genellikle*

V

vacant boş *bosh*
vacuum cleaner elektrik süpürgesi *elektrik sewpewrgesi*
valid geçerli *gecherli*
valuable değerli *de:erli*
valuables değerli eşya *de:erli eshya*
van kamyonet *kamyonet*
vanilla vanilya *vanilya*
vase vazo *vazo*
VAT KDV *kadeve*
vegan (etin yanısıra süt ve süt ürünleri de yemeyen) vejeteryan *(etin yanuhsuhra sewt ve sewt ewrewnleri de yemeyen) vezheteryan*
vegetarian *(adj.)* vejeteryan *vezheteryan*
vehicle araç *arach*
veil peçe *peche*
ventilation havalandırma *havalanduhrma*
vertigo baş dönmesi *bash dönmesi*
very çok *chok*
video video *video*
view manzara *manzara*
village köy *köy*
vinegar sirke *sirke*
vineyard bağ *ba:*
virgin bakire *ba:kire*
visa vize *vize*
to visit ziyaret etmek *ziya:ret etmek*
visitor ziyaretçi *ziya:retchi*
vitamin vitamin *vitamin*
voice ses *ses*
volleyball voleybol *voleybol*
voltage voltaj *voltazh*
to vomit kusmak *kusmak*

W

wafer gofret *gofret*
wage ücret *ewjret*
waist bel *bel*

to wait *(for)* (için) beklemek *(ichin) beklemek*

waiter/waitress garson *garson*

waiting room bekleme salonu *bekleme salonu*

Wales Galler *galler*

to walk, go for a walk yürümek, yürüyüşe çıkmak *yewrewmek, yewrewyewshe chuhkmak*

wall *(inside)* duvar *duvar (outside)* sur *sur*

wallet cüzdan *jewzdan*

to want istemek *istemek*

would like istemek *istemek*

war savaş *savash*

warm ılık *uhluhk*

to wash yıkamak *yuhkamak*

washable yıkanır *yuhkanuhr*

washing yıkama *yuhkama*

washing machine çamaşır makinesi *chamashuhr makinesi*

washing powder çamaşır tozu *chamashuhr tozu*

washing-up bulaşık *bulashuhk*

washing-up liquid deterjan *deterzhan*

watch saat *saat*

to watch seyretmek *seyretmek*

water su *su*

waterfall şelale *shela:le*

waterproof su geçirmez *su gechirmez*

water-skiing su kayağı *su kaya:uh*

wave dalga *dalga*

way *(path)* yol *yol*

» that way o taraf *o taraf*

» this way bu taraf *bu taraf*

way in giriş *girish*

way out çıkış *chuhkuhsh*

wax ağda *a:da*

we biz *biz*

weak *(drink)* hafif *hafif*

weather hava *hava*

weather forecast hava tahmini *hava tahmini*

web *(internet)* web *web*

web designer web tasarımcısı *web tasaruhmjuhsuh*

wedding düğün *dew:ewn*

week hafta *hafta*

weekday hafta arası *hafta arasuh*

weekend hafta sonu *hafta sonu*

weekly haftalık *haftaluhk*

to weigh tartmak *tartmak*

weight ağırlık *a:uhrluhk*

well iyi *iyi*

well done iyi pişmiş *iyi pishmish*

Welsh Galli *galli*

west batı *batuh*

western *(film)* batılı *batuhluh*

wet ıslak *uhslak*

wetsuit wetsuit *wetsuit*

what? ne *ne*

wheat buğday *bu:day*

wheel tekerlek *tekerlek*

wheelchair tekerlekli sandalye *tekerlekli sandalye*

when? ne zaman? *ne zaman*

where? nerede? *nerede*

which? hangi? *hangi*

which one? hangisi? *hangisi*

whisky viski *viski*

white beyaz *beyaz*

white coffee sütlü kahve *sewtlew kahve*

who? kim? *kim*

whole bütün *bewtewn*

wholemeal *(bread)* kepek ekmeği *kepek ekme:i*

why? niçin? *nichin*

wide geniş *genish*

widow/widower dul *dul*

wife karı *karuh*

wild yabani *yaba:ni*

to win kazanmak *kazanmak*

wind rüzgar *rewzgar*

windmill yeldeğirmeni *yelde:irmeni*

window *(shop)* vitrin *vitrin*

windscreen ön cam *ön jam*

to windsurf rüzgar sörfü *rewzgar sörfew*

windy rüzgarlı *rewzgarluh*

wine şarap *sharap*

wing kanat *kanat*
with ile *ile*
without -siz/-süz/-sız/-suz -*siz/-sewz/-suhz/-suz*
woman kadın *kaduhn*
wonderful çok güzel *chok gewzel*
wood tahta *tahta*
wool yün *yewn*
work iş *ish*
to work *(job)* çalışmak *chaluhshmak* *(function)* işlemek *ishlemek*
world dünya *dewnya*
worried endişeli *endisheli*
worse daha kötü *daha kötew*
worth: it's not worth it değer: değmez *de:er: de:mez*
would like istemek *istemek*
wound yara *yara*
to wrap *(up)* sarmak *sarmak*
wrist el bileği *el bile:i*
to write yazmak *yazmak*
writer yazar *yazar*
wrong yanlış *yanluhsh*

X

x-ray röntgen *röntgen*

Y

yacht yat *yat*
to yawn esnemek *esnemek*
year yıl *yuhl*
yellow sarı *saruh*
yes evet *evet*
yesterday dün *dewn*
yet henüz *henewz*
yoghurt yoğurt *yo:urt*
you *(formal)* siz, sizi *siz, sizi* *(singular)* sen, seni *sen, seni* *(plural)* siz, sizi *siz, sizi*
young genç *gench*
your sizin, senin *sizin, senin*
yours sizinki, seninki *sizinki, seninki*
youth gençlik *genchlik*
youth hostel gençlik yurdu *genchlik yurdu*

Z

zip fermuar *fermuar*
zoo hayvanat bahçesi *hayvanat bahchesi*

Turkish – English dictionary

A

acayip *aja:yip* strange
acele *ajele* haste, hurry
» acele etmek *ajele etmek* to hurry
acı *ajuh* bitter, hot (spicy)
acıkmak *ajuhkmak* to be hungry
» acıktım *ajuhktuhm* I am hungry
acımak *ajuhmak* to feel pain, to be
sorry for
acil *a:jil* urgent
» acil durum *a:jil durum* emergency
» acil servis *a:jil servis* emergency
service
aç *ach* hungry
açacak *achajak* bottle-opener
açık *achuhk* open
açlık *achluhk* hunger, famine
açmak *achmak* to open
ad *ad* name
ada *ada* island
adam *adam* man
adaptör *adaptör* adaptor
adet *a:det* custom, habit
adet ağrısı *a:det a:ruhsuh* period pain
adi *a:di* ordinary, common
adım *aduhm* step
adres *adres* address
affetmek *affetmek* to forgive, to pardon
affedersiniz *affedersiniz* I am sorry,
excuse me
afiyet olsun *a:fiyet olsun* enjoy your meal
ağ *a:* fishing net, web
ağaç *a:ach* tree
ağır *a:uhr* heavy, slow
ağırlık *a:uhrluhk* weight
ağız *a:uhz* mouth
ağlamak *a:lamak* to cry
ağrı *a:ruh* pain
ağrımak *a:ruhmak* to ache, to hurt
ahbap *ahbap* friend

ahçı *ahchuh* cook
ahize *ahize* receiver (telephone)
ahmak *ahmak* fool, stupid
aile *a:ile* family
ak *ak* white
akarsu *akarsu* river, stream
Akdeniz *akdeniz* the Mediterranean Sea
akıcı *akuhjuh* fluent
akıllı *akuhlluh* clever
akılsız *akuhlsuhz* stupid, silly
akıntı *akuhntuh* current (water)
akmak *akmak* to flow
akraba *akraba* relative, relation
akrep *akrep* scorpion
akşam *aksham* evening
akşamleyin *akshamleyin* in the evening
aktarma *aktarma* change (transport)
» aktarma yapmak *aktarma yapmak* to
change (train, etc.)
aktif *aktif* active
aktör *aktör* actor
akümülatör (akü) *akewmewlatör (akew)*
car battery
al *al* red
alafranga *alafranga* in the European
style
alarm *alarm* alarm
alaturka *alaturka* in the Turkish style
alçak *alchak* low
alerji *alerzhi* allergy
alet *a:let* tool, instrument
alfabe *alfabe* alphabet
alışveriş *aluhshverish* shopping
» alışverişe çıkmak *aluhshverishe*
chuhkmak to go shopping
alkol *alkol* alcohol
Allah *allah* God
allahaısmarladık *ala:smaladuhk* goodbye
almak *almak* to take
alo *alo* hello (on the phone)

alt *alt* bottom, under
altyazı *altyazuh* subtitle
altın *altuhn* gold
altüst *altewst* upside down
alyans *alyans* wedding ring
ama *ama* but
ambulans *ambulans* ambulance
ameliyat *ameliyat* surgery
ana *ana* mother *(colloquial)*
anahtar *anahtar* key
anarşi *anarshi* anarchy
anayol *anayol* main road
anıt *anuht* monument
ani *a:ni* sudden
anlam *anlam* meaning
anlamak *anlamak* to understand
anlaşma *anlashma* agreement
anlaştık *anlashtuhk* agreed
anlatmak *anlatmak* to explain
anne *anne* mother
anten *anten* aerial
antika *antika* antique
apartman *apartman* block of flats
apartman dairesi *apartman da:iresi* flat
apse *apse* abscess
aptal *aptal* silly, foolish
ara *ara* interval
araç *arach* vehicle
arasında *arasuhnda* between, among
arı *aruh* bee
arıza *a:ruhza* breakdown
arızalı *a:ruhzaluh* broken down, not functioning
arka *arka* back, reverse side
arkadaş *arkadash* friend
arkeolojik *arkeolozhik* archaeological land
armağan *arma:an* present
arpa *arpa* barley
artırmak *arturhrmak* to increase
asker *asker* soldier
askı *askuh* hanger
asmak *asmak* to hang
aşçı *ashchuh* cook

aşağıda *asha:uhda* below
aşı *ashuh* vaccination
aşık *a:shuhk* lover
» aşık olmak *a:shuhk olmak* to fall in love
aşırı doz *ashuhruh doz* overdose
aşk *ashk* love
at *at* horse
ateş *atesh* fire, fever
avukat *avukat* lawyer
ayakkabı *ayakkabuh* shoe
ayçiçeği *aychiche:i* sunflower
ayırtmak *ayuhrtmak* to reserve
ayna *ayna* mirror
aynı *aynuh* same
ayrı *ayruh* separate
ayrıntı *ayruhntuh* detail
az *az* a little, few
azami *a:zami* maximum

baba *baba* father
bagaj *bagazh* luggage, baggage
badem *ba:dem* almond
badem ezmesi *ba:dem ezmesi* marzipan
bağırmak *ba:uhrmak* to shout
bağırsak *ba:uhrsak* intestine
bahçe *bahche* garden
bahşiş *bahshish* tip
bakan *bakan* minister
bakkal *bakkal* grocer
baklava *baklava* pastry dessert
bakmak *bakmak* to look, to look after
bal *bal* honey
balayı *balayuh* honeymoon
balık *baluhk* fish
balkon *balkon* balcony
banka *banka* bank
bankamatik *bankamatik* cash machine, ATM
banliyö *banliyö* suburb
bardak *bardak* glass
barış *baruhsh* peace
basın *basuhn* the press, newspaper

banyo *banyo* bathroom
basit *basit* simple
baş *bash* head
baş ağrısı *bash a:ruhsuh* headache
başbakan *bashbakan* prime minister
başka *bashka* other, different
başkan *bashkan* president
başkent *bashkent* capital city
başlamak *bashlamak* to begin
batı *batuh* west
batmak *batmak* to sink
battaniye *batta:niye* blanket
bavul *bavul* suitcase
Bay *bay* Mr
Bayan *bayan* Mrs, Miss
bayat *bayat* stale
bayılmak *bayuhlmak* to faint
bayrak *bayrak* flag
bayram *bayram* festival
bazen *ba:zen* sometimes
bazı *ba:zuh* some
bebek *bebek* baby, doll
bebek maması *bebek mamasuh* baby
   food
bedava *beda:va* free *(of charge)*
beden *beden* size
beğenmek *be:enmek* to like
bekar *bekar* single
beklemek *beklemek* to wait
bekleme odası *bekleme odasuh* waiting
   room
belediye başkanı *belediye bashkanuh*
   mayor
belediye binası *belediye bina:suh* town
   hall
belge *belge* document
benzemek *benzemek* to look like
benzer *benzer* similar
benzin *benzin* petrol
benzin istasyonu *benzin istasyonu* petrol
   station
beraber *bera:ber* together
berber *berber* barber
beyaz *beyaz* white

beyaz zehir *beyaz zehir* cocaine
bıçak *buhchak* knife
bırakmak *buhrakmak* to leave, to quit
bırakılmak *buhrakuhlmak* to be left
bıyık *buhyuhk* moustache
bilet *bilet* ticket
biletçi *biletchi* ticket collector
bilet gişesi *bilet gishesi* ticket office,
   box office
bilezik *bilezik* bracelet
bilgi *bilgi* information
bilgisayar *bilgisayar* computer
bilmek *bilmek* to know
bina *bina* building
binicilik *binijilik* horse riding
biniş kartı *binish kartuh* boarding pass
bir *bir* one, a *(an)*
bira *bira* beer
biraz *biraz* a little
birinci *birinji* first
  » birinci sınıf *birinji suhnuhf* first class
birkaç *birkach* several, a few
bisiklet *bisiklet* bicycle
bisküvi *biskewvi* biscuit
bitirmek *bitirmek* to finish *(something)*
bitişik *bitishik* next to
bitki *bitki* plant
bizi *bizi* us
bizim *bizim* our
bluz *bluz* blouse
bodrum *bodrum* basement
boğaz *bo:az* throat
bomba *bomba* bomb
boş *bosh* empty
boşanmış *boshanmuhsh* divorced
boya *boya* paint
boyamak *boyamak* to paint, to decorate
bozuk *bozuk* out of order
bozuk para *bozuk para* small change
böcek *böjek* insect
broşür *broshewr* brochure
buçuk *buchuk* half *(as a number)*
bugün *bugewn* today
buhar *buhar* steam

bulaşık *bulashuhk* washing up
» bulaşık yıkamak *bulashuhk yuhkamak*
   to wash up
bulaşık makinesi *bulashuhk makinesi*
   dishwasher
bulmak *bulmak* to find
bulut *bulut* cloud
burada *burada* here
buz *buz* ice
buzdolabı *buzdolabuh* fridge
büfe *bewfe* kiosk (selling snacks)
büro *bewro* office
bütün *bewtewn* all
büyük *bewyewk* big, large
büyükelçilik *bewyewkelchilik* embassy
büyütmek *bewyewtmek* to enlarge

C

cadde *jadde* street
cam *jam* glass, window
cami *ja:mi* mosque
cankurtaran *jankurtaran* life guard,
   ambulance
canlı *janluh* alive, lively
can sıkıcı *jan suhkuhjuh* boring
casus *ja:sus* spy
caz *jaz* jazz
ceket *jeket* jacket
cenaze *jena:ze* funeral
cep *jep* pocket
cep telefonu *jep telefonu* mobile phone
cereyan *jereyan* draught, electric current
cevap *jevap* answer, response
ceza *jeza* fine, punishment
cezaevi *jezaevi* jail
ciddi *jiddi* serious
ciklet *jiklet* chewing gum
cilt *jilt* skin
cips *jips* chips
cüzdan *jewzdan* wallet, purse

Ç

çabuk *chabuk* quick
çabuk olmak *chabuk olmak* to hurry up

çadır *chaduhr* tent
çakı *chakuh* penknife
çakmak *chakmak* lighter
çalar saat *chalar saat* alarm clock
çalışmak *chaluhshmak* to work
çamaşır *chamashuhr* laundry
çamaşır makinesi *chamashuhr makinesi*
   washing machine
çanta *chanta* bag
çarpmak *charpmak* to crash
çarşaf *charshaf* sheet
çarşı *charshuh* market, bazaar, shops
çatal *chatal* fork
çatal bıçak *chatal buhchak* cutlery
çay *chay* tea
çekiç *chekich* hammer
çekmek *chekmek* to pull
çeşme *cheshme* fountain
çeyrek *cheyrek* quarter
çeviri *cheviri* translation
» çevirmek *chevirmek* to translate
çıkış *chuhkuhsh* exit
» çıkış yapmak *chuhkuhsh yapmak* to
   check out
çıkmak *chuhkmak* to come out
çıplak *chuhplak* nude
çiçek *chichek* flower
çift *chift* double, pair
çiftçi *chiftchi* farmer
çiftlik *chiftlik* farm
çiğ *chi:* raw
çikolata *chikolata* chocolate
çim *chim* grass
çirkin *chirkin* ugly
çocuk *chojuk* child
çocuk arabası *chojuk arabasuh* pram
çocuk bezi *chojuk bezi* nappy
çoğunluk *cho:unluk* majority
çok *chok* very, many, much
çorap *chorap* socks
çöp *chöp* litter, rubbish
çöp tenekesi *chöp tenekesi* dustbin
çünkü *chewnkew* because
çürük *chewrewk* rotten

D

dağ *da:* mountain
dağ kulübesi *da: kulübesi* hut
daha az *daha az* less
daha iyi *daha iyi* better
dahil *da:hil* included
daire *da:ire* flat
dakika *dakika* minute
dalga *dalga* wave
dalmak *dalmak* to dive
dam *dam* roof
damar *da:mar* vein
damat *damat* son-in-law
danışma *danuhshma* information
dans etmek *dans etmek* to dance
dar *dar* narrow
dava *da:va* trial
davet *da:vet* invitation
» davet etmek *da:vet etmek* to invite
da/de *da/de* also
dede *dede* grandfather
defter *defter* notebook
defol *defol* get out! go away!
değer *de:er* value
değerli *de:erli* valuable
değil *de:il* not
delikanlı *delikanluh* teenager *(male)*
demek *demek* to mean, to say
demir *demir* iron
demiryolu *demiryolu* railway
demlik *demlik* teapot
-de/-da/-te/-ta *-de/-da/-te/-ta* on, in, at
-den/-dan/-ten/-tan *-den/-dan/-ten/-tan* from
deniz *deniz* sea
deniz tutması *deniz tutmasuh* seasick
deprem *deprem* earthquake
dere *dere* stream, brook
dergi *dergi* magazine
derhal *derhal* immediately
deri *deri* leather
derin *derin* deep
dernek *dernek* society
ders *ders* lesson

devam etmek *devam etmek* to continue
dış *duhsh* external
dışarı *duhsharuh* out, outside
dışında *duhshuhnda* except
dibinde *dibinde* at the bottom of
diğer *di:er* other
dik *dik* step
dikkat *dikkat* attention, care
dikkatli *dikkatli* careful
dikkat etmek *dikkat etmek* to be careful
dikmek *dikmek* to sew, to plant
dil *dil* language, tongue
dilenci *dilenji* beggar
dilek *dilek* wish
dilemek *dilemek* to wish
dilim *dilim* slice
din *din* religion
dinlemek *dinlemek* to listen
dinlenmek *dinlenmek* to rest
dip *dip* bottom
dirsek *dirsek* elbow
dişçi *dishchi* dentist
diş fırçası *dish fuhrchasuh* toothbrush
doğa *do:a* nature
doğal *do:al* natural
doğu *do:u* east
doğum günü *do:um gewnew* birthday
dokunmak *dokunmak* to touch
doküman *dokewman* document
dolap *dolap* cupboard
doldurmak *doldurmak* to fill
dolgu *dolgu* filling
dolma *dolma* stuffed
dolma kalem *dolma kalem* pen
dolmuş *dolmush* shared taxi
dolu *dolu* full, engaged, busy
domates *domates* tomato
domuz *domuz* pig
dondurma *dondurma* ice-cream
donmuş *donmush* frozen
dosdoğru *dosdo:ru* straight ahead
dost *dost* friend
doymak *doymak* to be full *(food)*
döndürmek *döndewrmek* to turn around

dönmek *dönmek* to come back, to return
döşek *döshek* mattress
döviz *döviz* foreign currency
döviz kuru *döviz kuru* exchange rate
döviz bürosu *döviz bewrosu* foreign
    exchange office
dövme *dövme* tattoo
dövmek *dövmek* to beat
dudak *dudak* lip
dudak boyası *dudak boyasuh* lipstick
dul *dul* widow, widower
duman *duman* smoke
durak *durak* stop
durgun *durgun* still, calm
durmak *durmak* to stop
durum *durum* situation
duş *dush* shower
duvar *duvar* wall
duymak *duymak* to hear
düğme *dew:me* button, switch
düğün *dew:ewn* wedding
dükkan *dewkkan* shop
dün *dewn* yesterday
dünya *dewnya* world
dürüst *dewrewst* honest
düş *Dewsh* dream
  » düş görmek *dewsh görmek* to dream
düşman *dewshman* enemy
düşmek *dewshmek* to fall
düşünce *dewshewnje* thought
düşünmek *dewshewnmek* to think
düz *dewz* flat
düzenlemek *dewzenlemek* to organise
düzine *dewzine* dozen

E

-e/-a/-ye/-ya *-e/-a/-ye/-ya* to
eczane *ejzane* pharmacy, chemist
  » nöbetçi eczane *nöbetchi ejzane* duty
    chemist
efendim *efendim* sir, madam; I beg your
    pardon
Ege *ege* Aegean
eğer *e:er* if

eğlenmek *e:lenmek* to have fun
ek *ek* supplementary
ekmek *ekmek* bread
ekstra *ekstra* extra
ekşi *ekshi* sour
el bagajı *el bagazhuh* hand luggage
el çantası *el chantasuh* handbag
el feneri *el feneri* torch
el freni *el freni* handbrake
elbise *elbise* dress
elçilik *elchilik* embassy
eldiven *eldiven* glove
elektrik *elektrik* electricity
elektrik süpürgesi *elektrik sewpewrgesi*
    vacuum cleaner
elektrikli eşya *elektrikli eshya* electrical
    appliance
ellemek *ellemek* to touch
elma *elma* apple
elmas *elmas* diamond
emanet *ema:net* left luggage
emekli *emekli* pensioner
emin *emin* safe, sure
emniyet kemeri *emniyet kemeri* seat belt
en *en* most
en az *en az* at least, minimum
enfeksiyon *enfeksiyon* infection
engellemek *engellemek* to prevent
enişte *enishte* brother-in-law
eposta *eposta* email
erik *erik* plum
erkek *erkek* male, gents
erkek arkadaş *erkek arkadash* boyfriend
erkek kardeş *erkek kardesh* brother
erken *erken* early
esas *esas* main
eski *eski* old
esnasında *esnasuhnda* during
eş *esh* wife, husband
eşarp *esharp* scarf
eşek *eshek* donkey
eşek arısı *eshek aruhsuh* wasp
eşit *eshit* equal
eşofman *eshofman* tracksuit

eşya *eshya* furniture
et *et* meat
etek *etek* skirt
etiket *etiket* label
ev *ev* house
evet *evet* yes
evli *evli* married
evrak çantası *evrak chantasuh* briefcase
evvel *evvel* before

F

fabrika *fabrika* factory
fakat *fakat* but
fakir *fakir* poor
fare *fa:re* mouse
fark *fark* difference
fark etmez *fark etmez* it does not matter
fasulye *fasulye* beans
fatura *fatura* invoice
faks *faks* fax
faydalı *faydaluh* useful
fazla *fazla* too much, excessive
fazla bagaj *fazla bagazh* excess baggage
felaket *felaket* disaster
fener *fener* lighthouse, torch, lamp
feribot *feribot* car ferry
fermuar *fermuar* zip
fırça *fuhrcha* brush
fırın *fuhruhn* bakery, oven
fırtına *fuhrtuhna* storm
film *film* film
fincan *finjan* cup
fiyat *fiyat* price
flaş *flash* flash
flaş bellek *flash bellek* memory stick
flört etmek *flört etmek* to flirt
fotoğraf *foto:raf* photo
fotoğraf çekmek *foto:raf chekmek* to photograph
fotoğrafçı *foto:rafchuh* photographer
fotoğraf makinesi *foto:raf makinesi* camera
fön *fön* blow-dry
firen *firen* brake

G

Galler *galler* Wales
gar *gar* train station
garip *garip* strange
garson *garson* waiter
gazete *gazete* newspaper
gazete bayii *gazete bayii* newsagent
gazino *gazino* restaurant with show; open-air café
gazlı *gazluh* fizzy
gebe *gebe* pregnant
gece *geje* night
gece kulübü *geje kulewbew* nightclub
gece yarısı *geje yaruhsuh* midnight
gecikme *gejikme* delay
geç *gech* late
geç kalmak *gech kalmak* to be late
geçerli *gecherli* valid
geçit *gechit* crossing, pass
geçmek *gechmek* to pass, to overtake
gelecek *gelejek* future, next
gelenek *gelenek* custom, tradition
geleneksel *geleneksel* traditional
gelenler *gelenler* arrivals
gelin *gelin* daughter-in-law
geliştirmek *gelishtirmek* to develop
gelmek *gelmek* to come
gemi *gemi* ship
genç *gench* young
genellikle *genellikle* generally
geniş *genish* wide
gerçek *gerchek* truth, genuine
gerçekten *gerchekten* really
gerekli *gerekli* necessary
geri *geri* back, behind, backward
geri ödeme *geri ödeme* refund
getirmek *getirmek* to bring
gıda zehirlenmesi *guhda zehirlenmesi* food poisoning
gibi *gibi* like
gidilecek yer *gidilejek yer* destination
gidiş *gidish* single (ticket)
gidiş dönüş *gidish dönewsh* return (ticket)
giriş *girish* entrance

girmek *girmek* to enter
gitmek *gitmek* to go
giyim eşyası *giyim eshyasuh* clothing
giyinmek *giyinmek* to get dressed
giymek *giymek* to put on
gizli *gizli* secret
gök *gök* sky
gök gürültüsü *gök gewrewltewsew* thunder
gök kuşağı *gök kusha:uh* rainbow
göl *göl* lake
gölge *gölge* shadow
gölgede *gölgede* in the shade
gömlek *gömlek* shirt
göndermek *göndermek* to send
görmek *görmek* to see
göstermek *göstermek* to show
göz *göz* eye
gözlük *gözlewk* spectacles
gözlükçü *gözlewkchew* optician
gri *gri* grey
grip *grip* flu
grup *grup* group
güçlü *gewchlew* strong
güle güle *gewle gewle* goodbye
gülmek *gewlmek* to laugh
gülümsemek *gewlewmsemek* to smile
gülünç *gewlewnch* ridiculous
gümrük *gewmrewk* customs
gümrüksüz *gewmrewksewz* duty free
gümüş *gewmewsh* silver
gün *gewn* day
günaydın *gewnayduhn* good morning
günce *gewnje* diary
güncel *gewnjel* current
gündelik *gewndelik* daily
güneş *gewnesh* sun
güneş banyosu *gewnesh banyosu* sunbathing
güneşli *gewneshli* sunny
güneş yanığı *gewnesh yanuh:uh* sunburn
güney *gewney* south
gürültü *gewrewltew* noise
güvenli *gewvenli* safe

güvenmek *gewvenmek* to trust
güverte *gewverte* deck
güzel *gewzel* beautiful, nice

H

haber *haber* news
hacim *hajim* volume
hafıza kartı *ha:fuhza kartuh* memory card
hafif *hafif* light
hafta *hafta* week
hafta sonu *hafta sonu* weekend
haklı olmak *hakluh olmak* to be right
halat *halat* rope
halı *haluh* carpet
Haliç *halich* Golden Horn
halk *halk* people
hamam *hamam* Turkish bath
hamamböceği *hamamböje:i* cockroach
hamile *ha:mile* pregnant
hangi *hangi* which
hangisi *hangisi* which one
hanım *hanuhm* lady
hap *hap* pill
hapishane *hapisha:ne* prison
hapşırmak *hapshuhrmak* to sneeze
harabe *hara:be* ruin
harcamak *harjamak* to spend
hardal *hardal* mustard
hareket etmek *hareket etmek* to move
hariç *ha:rich* except, external
harika *ha:rika* great
harita *harita* map
hasta *hasta* ill, patient
hastabakıcı *hastabakuhjuh* nurse
hastalık *hastaluhk* disease
hastane *hastane* hospital
hata *hata* mistake
hatıra *ha:tuhra* souvenir, memoirs
hatırlamak *hatuhrlamak* to remember
hatta *hatta* even
hava *hava* air, weather
havaalanı *havaalanuh* airport
hava tahmini *hava tahmini* weather forecast

havayolu *havayolu* airline
havlu *havlu* towel
havuç *havuch* carrot
hayat *hayat* life
hayır *hayuhr* no
hayvan *hayvan* animal
hayvanat bahçesi *hayvanat bahchesi* zoo
hazımsızlık *hazuhmsuhzluhk* indigestion
hediye *hediye* present *(gift)*
hekim *hekim* doctor
hela *hela:* lavatory
hemen *hemen* immediately
hemşire *hemshire* nurse
hemzemin geçit *hemzemin gechit* level
  crossing
henüz *henewz* just, yet
hep *hep* all, always
hepimiz *hepimiz* all of us
hepsi *hepsi* all of it, them
her *her* each, every
herkes *herkes* everyone
her şey *her shey* everything
her zaman *her zaman* always
hesap *hesap* bill
hesap makinesi *hesap makinesi* calculator
heyecan *heyejan* excitement
heykel *heykel* statue
hıçkırık *huhchkuhruhk* hiccups
hırka *huhrka* cardigan
hırsız *huhrsuhz* thief
hırsızlık *huhrsuhzluhk* theft
hız *huhz* speed
hızlı *huhzluh* fast
hiç (bir şey) *hich (bir shey)* nothing
hiç kimse *hich kimse* nobody
hijyenik bağ *hizhyenik ba:* sanitary towel
hikaye *hika:ye* story
hindi *hindi* turkey
his *his* feeling
hisar *hisar* fortress
hissetmek *hissetmek* to feel
hizmet *hizmet* service
» hizmet etmek *hizmet etmek* to serve
horlamak *horlamak* to snore

hostes *hostes* stewardess
hoş *hosh* fine, nice
hoş geldiniz *hosh geldiniz* welcome
hoşlanmak *hoshlanmak* to like
hükümet *hewkew:met* government
hürriyet *hewrriyet* freedom

I

ılık *uhluhk* warm
ırza geçmek *uhrza gechmek* to rape
ısırmak *uhsuhrmak* to bite
ısıtma *uhsuhtma* heating
ıslak *uhslak* wet
ısmarlamak *uhsmarlamak* to order
ıspanak *uhspanak* spinach
ışık *uhshuhk* light
ızgara *uhzgara* grilled

İ

iade etmek *iade etmek* to give back
iç *Ich* inside
iç çamaşırı *ich chamashuhruh* underwear
içeri *icheri* inside
için *ichin* for
içecek *ichejek* drink
içecek su *ichejek su* drinking water
içmek *ichmek* to drink
iğne *i:ne* needle
iğne olmak *i:ne olmak* to have an
  injection
iğrenç *i:rench* disgusting
ikamet *ika:met* residence
iklim *iklim* climate
ilaç *ilach* medicine
böcek ilacı *böjek ilajuh* insect repellent
ile *ile* with, by
ileri *ileri* forward
ilgi *ilgi* attention, care
ilginç *ilginch* interesting
ilişki *ilishki* contact
ilk yardım *ilk yarduhm* first aid
imdat! *imdat* help!
imza *imza:* signature
imzalamak *imza:lamak* to sign

inanmak *inanmak* to believe
ince *inje* thin
incitmek *injitmek* to hurt
indirim *indirim* reduction, discount
indirimli satış *indirimli satuhs* sale
inek *inek* cow
inmek *inmek* to get off
insan *insan* man, mankind
internet sitesi *internet sitesi* website
ip *ip* string
ipek *ipek* silk
iplik *iplik* thread
iptal etmek *iptal etmek* to cancel
iri *iri* large, big
İsa *isa* Jesus
ishal *ishal* diarrhoea
iskele *iskele* pier
iskemle *iskemle* chair
İslam *islam* Islam
İslamik *islamik* Islamic
İstanbul Boğazı *istanbul bo:azuh*
   Bosphorus
istasyon *istasyon* station
istemek *istemek* to want, to request
iş *ish* job, business, work
işitme cihazı *ishitme jihazuh* hearing aid
işitmek *ishitmek* to hear
işlek *ishlek* busy
işsiz *ishsiz* unemployed
iştah *ishtah* appetite
itfaiye *itfaiye* fire brigade
itmek *itmek* to push
iyi *iyi* good, well
iyimser *iyimser* optimistic
izin *izin* permission, leave
izin vermek *izin vermek* to allow

J

jambon *zhambon* ham
jilet *zhilet* razor blade
jandarma *zhandarma* military police
jelatin *zhelatin* gelatine
jest *zhest* gesture
jöle *zhöle* jelly

K

kaba *kaba* rude
kabız *kabuhz* constipation
kabin memuru *kabin me:muru* steward
kabuk *kabuk* shell
kabul etmek *kabul etmek* to accept
kaburga *kaburga* rib
kaç *kach* how many, how much
kaçak *kachak* leak
kadar *kadar* as
kadın *kaduhn* woman
kağıt *ka:uht* paper
kağıt mendil *ka:uht mendil* tissues
kahvaltı *kahvaltuh* breakfast
kahve *kahve* coffee
kahverengi *kahverengi* brown
kakao *kakao* hot chocolate
kalabalık *kalabaluhk* crowd, crowded
kaldırım *kalduhruhm* pavement
kale *kale* castle
kalem *kalem* pencil
kalın *kaluhn* thick
kalite *kalite* quality
kalkış *kalkuhsh* departure
kalkmak *kalkmak* to take off, to get up
kalmak *kalmak* to stay
kalorifer *kalorifer* central heating
kalp *kalp* heart
kalp krizi *kalp krizi* heart attack
kamara *kamara* cabin
kambiyo *kambiyo* foreign exchange
   counter
kamyon *kamyon* lorry
kamyonet *kamyonet* van
kan *kan* blood
kan grubu *kan grubu* blood type
kanamak *kanamak* to bleed
kanun *ka:nun* law
kapak *kapak* lid
kapalı *kapaluh* closed
kapamak *kapamak* to switch off
kapatmak *kapatmak* to close
kapı *kapuh* door
kaplıca *kapluhja* spa

kaptan *kaptan* captain
kar *kar* snow
kara *kara* black
Karadeniz *karadeniz* Black Sea
karanlık *karanluhk* dark
karar *karar* decision
karar vermek *karar vermek* to decide
karınca *karuhnja* ant
karışık *karuhshuhk* mixed
karıştırmak *karuhshtuhrmak* to mix
karides *karides* prawn
karşı *karshuh* against, opposite
karşılamak *karshuhlamak* to meet
kart *kart* card
kartpostal *kartpostal* postcard
kasa *kasa* cash desk, strongbox
kasap *kasap* butcher, butcher's
kase *ka:se* bowl
kaset *kaset* cassette
kaş *kash* eyebrow
kaşık *kashuhk* spoon
kaşıntı *kashuhntuh* itch
kat *kat* floor
kavga *kavga* fight
kavşak *kavshak* junction
kaya *kaya* rock
kayak *kayak* skiing
kaybetmek *kaybetmek* to lose
kaybolmak *kaybolmak* to get lost, to
    disappear
kaygan *kaygan* slippery
kayık *kayuhk* rowing boat
kayıp *kayuhp* lost
kayıp eşya *kayuhp eshya* lost property
kayıt *kayuht* register, registration
kaymak *kaymak* to slide, to skid
kaynana *kaynana* mother-in-law
kaynamış *kaynamuhsh* boiled
kaynar su *kaynar su* boiling water
kaza *kaza:* accident
kazak *kazak* jersey, sweater
kazanmak *kazanmak* to win, to earn
kebap *kebap* kebab
keçi *kechi* goat

kedi *kedi* cat
kek *kek* cake
kel *kel* bald
kelebek *kelebek* butterfly
kelime *kelime* word
kemer *kemer* belt
kemik *kemik* bone
kenar *kenar* edge
kendi *kendi* him, her, itself; own
kepenk *kepenk* shutters
kere *kere* time(s)
kerpeten *kerpeten* pliers
kesik *kesik* cut, cut off
kesmek *kesmek* to cut
kestane *kesta:ne* chestnut
kestirme *kestirme* shortcut
kılçık *kuhlchuhk* fishbone
kır *kuhr* countryside
kırık *kuhruhk* broken
kırmak *kuhrmak* to break
kırmızı *kuhrmuhzuh* red
kısa *kuhsa* short
kıskanç *kuhskanch* jealous
kış *kuhsh* winter
kıyı *kuhyuh* coast
kıyma *kuhyma* mince
kız *kuhz* girl
kız arkadaş *kuhz arkadash* girlfriend
kızartmak *kuhzartmak* to fry
kızıl *kuhzuhl* red
kibrit *kibrit* match
kilim *kilim* flat-weave rug
kilise *kilise* church
kilit *kilit* lock
kim *kim* who
kime *kime* to whom
kimin *kimin* whose
kimlik *kimlik* identity
kimlik kartı *kimlik kartuh* identity card
kira *kira:* rent
kiralamak *kira:lamak* to rent
kiralık *kira:luhk* for hire, to let
kirli *kirli* dirty, polluted

Kitab-ı Mukaddes *kitab-uh mukaddes*
Bible
kitapçı *kitapchuh* bookstore
klima *klima* air-conditioning
klimalı *klimaluh* air-conditioned
koca *koja* husband, huge
kod *kod* code
koklamak *koklamak* to sniff
kokmak *kokmak* to give off a smell
koku *koku* smell, perfume
kol *kol* arm, handle
kol saati *kol saati* watch
kolay *kolay* easy
koli *koli* package
kolye *kolye* necklace
kompartıman *kompartuhman*
compartment
komşu *komshu* neighbour
konser *konser* concert
konserve *konserve* tinned food
konsolosluk *konsolosluk* consulate
kontak lens *kontak lens* contact lens
kontrol etmek *kontrol etmek* to check
konuk *konuk* guest
konuşmak *konushmak* to speak; to talk
korku *korku* fear
korkunç *korkunch* horrible
korumak *korumak* to protect
koşmak *koshmak* to run
kova *kova* bucket
koymak *koymak* to put
koyun *koyun* sheep
köpek *köpek* dog
köprü *köprew* bridge
kör *kör* blind
köşe *köshe* corner
kötü *kötew* bad
köy *köy* village
krem şanti *krem shanti* whipped cream
krema *krema* cream
kuaför *kuaför* hairdresser
kullanmak *kullanmak* to use
kum *kum* sand
kumanda *kumanda* remote control

kumaş *kumash* fabric
Kuran *kur an* Qur'an
kuru *kuru* dry
kuru temizleyici *kuru temizleyiji* dry-
cleaner
kuş *kush* bird
kuşet *kushet* couchette
kutu *kutu* box
kuyruk *kuyruk* tail, queue
kuyumcu *kuyumju* jeweller's
kuzen *kuzen* cousin
kuzey *kuzey* north
kuzu *kuzu* lamb
küçük *kewchewk* small
külot *kewlot* underpants
külotlu çorap *kewlotlu chorap* tights
kül *kewl* ash
kül tablası *kewl tablasuh* ashtray
küpe *kewpe* earring
kütüphane *kewtewphane* library

L

lamba *lamba* lamp
lastik *lastik* rubber, tyre
lavabo *lavabo* basin
lazım *lazuhm* necessary, needed
-le/-la *-le/-la* with, by
leke *leke* stain
lezzetli *lezzetli* delicious
-li/-lü/-lı/-lu *-li/-lew/-luh/-lu* with,
containing
likör *likör* liqueur
liman *liman* port, harbour
limon *limon* lemon
lisan *lisan* language
lokanta *lokanta* restaurant
lokum *lokum* Turkish delight
Londra *londra* London
lütfen *lewtfen* please

M

maç *mach* match *(sports)*
maden suyu *maden suyu* mineral water
mağara *ma:ara* cave

makarna *makarna* pasta
makas *makas* scissors
makbuz *makbuz* receipt
makyaj *makyazh* make-up
makyaj malzemesi *makyazh malzemesi* cosmetics
mal *mal* property
manav *manav* greengrocer
Manş Denizi *mansh denizi* English Channel
manzara *manzara* scenery
martı *martuh* seagull
masa *masa* table
masa örtüsü *masa örtewsew* tablecloth
masa tenisi *masa tenisi* table tennis
masaj *masazh* massage
mavi *ma:vi* blue
mayo *mayo* swimsuit
mazot *mazot* diesel
mektup *mektup* letter
-meli, -malı *-meli, -maluh* must, have to
meme *meme* breast
memnun *memnun* glad
memnun oldum *memnun oldum* I am pleased, pleased to meet you
memur *me:mur* official, civil servant
mendil *mendil* handkerchief
merak *merak* hobby
merdiven *merdiven* ladder, stairs
merhaba *merhaba:* hello
mesela *mesela:* for example
meslek *meslek* profession
meşgul *meshgul* engaged
metro *metro* underground
meydan *meydan* square
meyve *meyve* fruit
mezarlık *mezarluhk* cemetery
mobilya *mobilya* furniture
moda *moda* fashion
mola *mola* pause, rest
mor *mor* purple
motosiklet *motosiklet* motorcycle
mum *mum* candle
musluk *musluk* tap, washbasin

mutfak *mutfak* kitchen
mutlu *mutlu* happy
mücevher *mewjevher* jewel
mücevherat *mewjevhera:t* jewellery
mümkün *mewmkewn* possible
mürettebat *mewretteba:t* crew
mushil *mushil* laxative
Müslüman *mewslewman* Muslim
müthiş *mewthish* terrific
müze *mewze* museum
müzik *mewzik* music

N

nakit *nakit* cash
namaz *namaz* muslim prayer
nargile *nargile* hookah, waterpipe
nasıl *nasuhl* how
nazik *na:zik* polite, kind
ne *ne* what
›› ne haber? *ne haber* how are things?
›› ne kadar ? *ne kadar* how much?
›› ne zaman ? *ne zaman* when?
ne ... ne *ne ... ne* neither ... nor
neden *neden* why
nedeniyle *nedeniyle* because of
nefes *nefes* breath
nefes almak *nefes almak* to breathe
nefis *nefis* delicious, excellent
nehir *nehir* river
nemlendirici *nemlendiriji* moisturiser
nerede *nerede* where
niçin *nichin* why
Noel *noel* Christmas
sayı *sayuh* number

O

o *o* he, she, it; that
Ocak *ojak* January
ocak *ojak* cooker
oda *oda* room
oğlan *o:lan* boy
oğul *o:ul* son
okul *okul* school
okumak *okumak* to read

olgun *olgun* ripe

olmak *olmak* to be, to become, to happen

ona *ona* to him, to her, to it

onu *onu* him, her, it

orada *orada* there

orası *orasuh* there, that place

ordu *ordu* army

orman *orman* forest

orta *orta* middle, medium

Osmanlı *osmanluh* Ottoman

ot *ot* grass

otobüs *otobews* bus

» otobüs durağı *otobews dura:uh* bus-stop

otogar *otogar* coach station

otomobil *otomobil* car

otopark *otopark* car park

otostop *otostop* hitchhike

otoyol *otoyol* motorway

oturacak yer *oturajak yer* seat

oturmak *oturmak* sit down, reside

oturma odası *oturma odasuh* living room

oynamak *oynamak* to play (games)

oyun *oyun* play, game

oyuncak *oyunjak* toy

Ö

öbür gün *öbewr gewn* the day after tomorrow

ödemek *ödemek* to pay

ödemeli *ödemeli* reverse charge call

ödünç *ödewnch* borrowed

» ödünç almak *ödewnch almak* to borrow

» ödünç vermek *ödewnch vermek* to lend

öğle *ö:le* midday

öğleden sonra *ö:leden sonra* in the afternoon

öğle yemeği *ö:le yeme:i* lunch

öğlenleyin *ö:lenleyin* at midday

öğrenci *ö:renji* student

öğrenmek *ö:renmek* to learn

öğretmek *ö:retmek* to teach

öğretmen *ö:retmen* teacher

öksürük *öksewrewk* cough

ölçü *ölchew* measurement

öldürmek *öldewrmek* to kill

ölmek *ölmek* to die

ölü *ölew* dead

ön *ön* front

önce *önje* before, ago

önemli *önemli* important

önemsiz *önemsiz* unimportant

öneri *öneri* suggestion

önermek *önermek* to suggest, to advise

öpmek *öpmek* to kiss

öpücük *öpewjewk* kiss

ördek *ördek* duck

örgü *örgew* knitting

örnek *örnek* example

örneğin *örne:in* for example

örümcek *örewmjek* spider

özür *özewr* apology

» özür dilemek *özewr dilemek* to apologise

» özür dilerim *özewr dilerim* I am sorry

özürlü *özewrlew* disabled

P

pahalı *pahaluh* expensive

paket *paket* parcel

paketleme *paketleme* to wrap up

palto *palto* overcoat

pamuk *pamuk* cotton

pansiyon *pansiyon* guest house

pantolon *pantolon* trousers

para *para* money

para üstü *para ewstew* change (money)

para iadesi *para iadesi* refund

parça *parcha* piece, part

pardon *pardon* excuse me

park *park* park

» park etmek *park etmek* to park

parlak *parlak* gloss

parmak *parmak* finger

parmaklık *parmakluhk* fence, railings

Paskalya *paskalya* Easter
pasta *pasta* cake, gateau
pastane *pasta:ne* café, cake shop
patates *patates* potato
patlak *patlak* burst, punctured
patlıcan *patluhjan* aubergine
patron *patron* boss
pay *pay* share
paylaşmak *paylashmak* to share
pazar *pazar* market
peçete *pechete* napkin
pek *pek* very
pek az *pek az* very little
pek değil *pek de:il* not much
pembe *pembe* pink
pencere *penjere* window
perde *perde* curtain
perhiz *perhiz* diet
peron *peron* platform
peşin *peshin* in advance
peynir *peynir* cheese
pil *pil* battery
pipo *pipo* pipe
pişirmek *pishirmek* to cook
pişmiş *pishmish* cooked
plaj *plazh* beach
plaka *plaka* number plate
plan *plan* plan, map
polis *polis* police
politika *politika* politics
pop müzik *pop mewzik* pop music
porsiyon *porsiyon* portion
portatif *portatif* portable
posta *posta* post
postacı *postajuh* postman
postalamak *postalamak* to post
postane *posta:ne* post office
prens *prens* prince
prenses *prenses* princess
prezervatif *prezervatif* condom
priz *priz* socket
program *program* programme
protez *protez* denture
pul *pul* stamp

puro *puro* cigar
puset *puset* push-chair

R

radyatör *radyatör* radiator
raf *raf* shelf
rahat *rahat* comfortable
rahatsız *rahatsuhz* uncomfortable,
    unwell
rahip *ra:hip* priest
rakip *rakip* rival
randevu *randevu* appointment
reçel *rechel* jam
reçete *rechete* prescription
rehber *rehber* guide
renk *renk* colour
resim *resim* picture
resmi *resmi* official
resmi tatil *resmi ta:til* public holiday
rezervasyon *rezervasyon* reservation
rıhtım *ruhhtuhm* quay
rimel *rimel* mascara
roman *roman* novel
rota *rota* route
römork *römork* trailer
röntgen *röntgen* X-ray
ruj *ruzh* lipstick
rüya *rewya* dream
rüzgar *rewzgar* wind

S

saat *saat* hour, clock, watch
saat kaç? *saat kach* what time is it?
sabah *sabah* morning
sabun *sabun* soap
saç *sach* hair
saç kurutma makinesi *sach kurutma
    makinesi* hairdryer
sadece *sa:deje* only
saf *saf* pure
sağ *sa:* right, alive
sağır *sa:uhr* deaf
sağlığınıza! *sa:luh:uhnuhza* your health!
sağlıklı *sa:luhkluh* healthy

sağol *sa:ol* **thanks**

sahil *sa:hil* **shore, coast**

sahip *sa:hip* **owner**

sahip olmak *sa:hip olmak* **to possess**

sahte *sahte* **false, imitation**

sakal *sakal* **beard**

sakin *sa:kin* **calm, quiet**

sakinleşmek *sa:kinleshmek* **to calm down**

sakinleştirici *sa:kinleshtiriji* **tranquilliser**

saklamak *saklamak* **to hide, to keep**

salata *salata* **salad**

saldırgan *salduhrgan* **aggressive, aggressor**

saldırı *salduhruh* **attack**

salyangoz *salyangoz* **snail**

saman nezlesi *saman nezlezi* **hay fever**

sanat galerisi *sanat galerisi* **art gallery**

sanatçı *sanatchuh* **artist**

sanayi *sana:yi* **industry**

saralı *saraluh* **epileptic**

saray *saray* **palace**

sargı *sarguh* **bandage**

sarhoş *sarhosh* **drunk**

» sarhoş olmak *sarhosh olmak* **to get drunk**

sarı *saruh* **yellow**

sarışın *saruhshuhn* **blonde**

sarmak *sarmak* **to wrap**

sarımsak *saruhmsak* **garlic**

satılık *satuhluhk* **for sale**

satın almak *satuhn almak* **to buy**

satış *satuhsh* **sale**

satmak *satmak* **to sell**

savaş *savash* **war, battle**

sayfa *sayfa* **page**

saz *saz* **Turkish string instrument**

sebze *sebze* **vegetable**

seçmek *sechmek* **to choose**

sel *sel* **flood**

selam! *selam* **greetings!**

semaver *sema:ver* **samovar**

sempatik *sempatik* **appealing** *(person)*

semt *semt* **district**

sen *sen* **you** *(as subject)*

seni *seni* **you** *(as object)*

sepet *sepet* **basket**

serbest *serbest* **free**

sergi *sergi* **exhibition**

serin *serin* **cool**

sert *sert* **hard**

servis *servis* **service**

» servis (ücreti) dahildir *servis (ewjreti) da:hildir* **service (charge) is included**

servis istasyonu *servis istasyonu* **garage**

ses *ses* **voice**

sessiz *sessiz* **silent**

sessizlik *sessizlik* **silence**

sevgi *sevgi* **love**

sevişmek *sevishmek* **to make love**

sevmek *sevmek* **to love**

seyahat *seya:hat* **travel**

seyahat acentası *seya:hat ajentasuh* **travel agent's**

seyahat çeki *seyahat cheki* **traveller's cheque**

seyirci *seyirji* **audience, spectator**

seyretmek *seyretmek* **to watch**

sıcak *suhjak* **hot**

sıcaklık *suhjakluhk* **heat, temperature**

sıfır *suhfuhr* **zero**

sığ *suh:* **shallow**

sık *suhk* **frequent**

» sık sık *suhk suhk* **often**

sıkı *suhkuh* **tight**

sıkıcı *suhkuhjuh* **boring**

sıkışmak *suhkuhshmak* **to get stuck**

sınıf *suhnuhf* **class**

sınır *suhnuhr* **border, limit**

sıra *suhra* **row**

sırasında *suhrasuhnda* **during**

sırt *suhrt* **back**

sırt çantası *suhrt chantasuh* **backpack**

sızmak *suhzmak* **to leak**

sigara *sigara* **cigarette**

sigara içilmez *sigara ichilmez* **no smoking**

sigara içmek *sigara ichmek* **to smoke**

silah *silah* **weapon**

silmek *silmek* **to erase, to wipe**

SİM kart *sim kart* SIM card
sinek *sinek* fly
sinema *sinema* cinema
sinirli *sinirli* nervous
sinyal *sinyal* signal
sipariş *siparish* order
sirke *sirke* vinegar
sis *sis* fog
sivrisinek *sivrisinek* mosquito
siyah *siyah* black
siyah beyaz *siyah beyaz* black and white
siz *siz* you
soğan *so:an* onion
soğuk *so:uk* cold
sokak *sokak* street
sol *sol* left
solak *solak* left-handed
son *son* end
sonra *sonra* then, afterwards
sonradan *sonradan* later
sormak *sormak* to ask *(question)*
soru *soru* question
sorumlu *sorumlu* responsible
sorun *sorun* problem
soyadı *soyaduh* surname
soymak *soymak* to peel, to undress
söndürmek *söndewrmek* to blow out, put out *(fire, etc.)*
sörf yapmak *sörf yapmak* to surf
söylemek *söylemek* to say
söz *söz* words, promise
söz vermek *söz vermek* to promise
sözel *sözel* oral
spor *spor* sports
su *su* water
suni *su:ni* artificial
susamak *susamak* to be thirsty
›› susadım *susaduhm* I am thirsty
sünnet *sewnnet* circumcision
süpürge *sewpewrge* broom
sürahi *sewra:hi* jug
süre *sewre* period
sürmek *sewrmek* to drive, to last
sürpriz *sewrpriz* surprise

sürücü *sewrewjew* driver
sürücü belgesi *sewrewjew belgesi* driving licence
süt *sewt* milk
sütlü *sewtlew* with milk
sütsüz *sewtsewz* without milk
sütun *sewtun* column, pillar
sütyen *sewtyen* bra

Ş

şahane *sha:ha:ne* wonderful
şair *sha:ir* poet
şaka *shaka* joke
şal *shal* shawl
şamandra *shamandra* buoy
şampuan *shampuan* shampoo
şans *shans* luck
›› iyi şanslar! *iyi shanslar* good luck!
şapka *shapka* hat
şarap *sharap* wine
şarj cihazı *sharzh jihazuh* charger *(telephone)*
şarkı *sharkuh* song
şarkı söylemek *sharkuh söylemek* to sing
şaşırmak *shashuhrmak* to be surprised
şato *shato* castle
şehir *shehir* city, town
›› şehir merkezi *shehir merkezi* city centre
şeker *sheker* sugar
şeker hastası *sheker hastasuh* diabetic
şemsiye *shemsiye* umbrella
şerefe! *sherefe* cheers!
şey *shey* thing
şezlong *shezlong* deck chair
şifre *shifre* PIN code
şikayet *shika:yet* complaint
şikayet etmek *shika:yet etmek* to complain
şilte *shilte* mattress
şimdi *shimdi* now
şirket *shirket* company
şiş *shish* swelling, skewer
şişe *shishe* bottle

şişman *shishman* fat

şoför *shoför* chauffeur

şoför ehliyeti *shoför ehliyeti* driving licence

şort *short* shorts

şu *shu* that

şunlar *shunlar* those

T

taahhütlü *taahhewtlew* registered (mail)

tabak *tabak* plate

tabiki *tabi:ki* of course

tabldot *tabldot* set menu

tahta *tahta* wood

tahlil *tahlil* test (blood, urine etc.)

takım *takuhm* team, set

takip etmek *ta:kip etmek* to follow

takvim *takvim* calendar

talep *talep* demand

talih *ta:lih* luck

tamam *tamam* OK, all right

tamamlamak *tamamlamak* to complete

tamir etmek *ta:mir etmek* to repair

Tam *tam* whole

tam zamanında *tam zamanuhnda* on time

tanık *tanuhk* witness

Tanrı *tanruh* God

tansiyon *tansiyon* blood pressure

tarife *ta:rife* timetable, recipe

tarih *ta:rih* date, rate

tarla *tarla* field

tas *tas* bowl

taş *tash* stone

taşımak *tashuhmak* to carry

taşıt *tashuht* vehicle

tat *tat* flavour

tatil *ta:til* holiday

tatlı *tatluh* sweet, dessert

tatmak *tatmak* to taste

tava *tava* fried, frying pan

tavan *tavan* ceiling

tavsiye *tavsiye* recommendation

» tavsiye etmek *tavsiye etmek* to recommend

tavşan *tavshan* rabbit

tavuk *tavuk* chicken

taze *ta:ze* fresh

tazminat *tazmi:nat* compensation

tebrik *tebrik* congratulations

» tebrik etmek *tebrik etmek* to congratulate

tecrübeli *tejrewbeli* experienced

tehlike *tehlike* danger

tehlikeli *tehlikeli* dangerous

tek kişilik *tek kishilik* single (bed, room, etc.)

Tekel bayii *tekel bayii* kind of off-licence

tekerlek *tekerlek* wheel

tekerlekli sandalye *tekerlekli sandalye* wheelchair

teklif etmek *teklif etmek* to propose

tekrar *tekrar* again

tekrarlamak *tekrarlamak* to repeat

teleferik *teleferik* cable-car

telefon *telefon* telephone

» telefon etmek *telefon etmek* to phone

» telefon kodu *telefon kodu* dialling code

tembel *tembel* lazy

temiz *temiz* clean

temizlemek *temizlemek* to clean

temizlikçi *temizlikchi* cleaner

temsilci *temsilji* representative

tencere *tenjere* saucepan

tenzilat *tenzilat* reduction

tepe *tepe* hill

tercih *terjih* preference

» tercih etmek *terjih etmek* to prefer

terlemek *terlemek* to sweat

terlik *terlik* slipper

terzi *terzi* tailor

tıkaç *tuhkach* plug

tıklamak *tuhklamak* to click

teşekkür etmek *teshekkewr etmek* to thank

» teşekkür ederim *teshekkewr ederim* thank you

» teşekkürler *teshekkewrler* thanks

teyp *teyp* **tape**
tıkamak *tuhkamak* **to block**
tıkalı *tuhkaluh* **blocked**
tıraş olmak *tuhrash olmak* **to shave**
tırnak *tuhrnak* **nail**
tırnak cilası *tuhrnak jilasuh* **nail varnish**
tirbuşon *tirbushon* **corkscrew**
tişört *tishört* **T-shirt**
tiyatro *tiyatro* **theatre**
top *top* **ball**
toplantı *toplantuh* **meeting**
toprak *toprak* **earth**
topuk *topuk* **heel**
tornavida *tornavida* **screwdriver**
torun *torun* **grandchild**
trafik *trafik* **traffic**
tren *tren* **train**
tuğla *tu:la* **brick**
turuncu *turunju* **orange colour**
tutmak *tutmak* **to hold, to rent**
tutuklamak *tutuklamak* **to arrest**
tutuşmak *tutushmak* **to fire**
tutuşturmak *tutushturmak* **to set fire to**
tuvalet *tuvalet* **toilet**
tuvalet kağıdı *tuvalet ka:uhduh* **toilet paper**
tuz *tuz* **salt**
tükenmez kalem *tewkenmez kalem* **ballpoint pen**
tüm *tewm* **all**
tümüyle *tewmewyle* **altogether**
tünel *tewnel* **tunnel**
Türk kahvesi *tewrk kahvesi* **Turkish coffee**
tütün *tewtewn* **tobacco**

U

ucuz *ujuz* **cheap**
uçak *uchak* **aeroplane**
uçak seferi *uchak seferi* **flight**
uçmak *uchmak* **to fly**
ufak *ufak* **small**
ulus *ulus* **nation**
uluslararası *uluslararasuh* **international**
ummak *ummak* **to hope**

umut *umut* **hope**
un *un* **flour**
unutmak *unutmak* **to forget**
utangaç *utangach* **shy**
uyanık *uyanuhk* **awake**
uyanmak *uyanmak* **to wake up**
uyku *uyku* **sleep**
  ›› uykum geldi *uykum geldi* **I am sleepy**
uyku ilacı *uyku ilajuh* **sleeping pill**
uyku tulumu *uyku tulumu* **sleeping bag**
uyruk *uyruk* **nationality**
uyumak *uyumak* **to sleep**
uyuşturucu *uyushturuju* **drugs**
uzak *uzak* **far**
uzaklık *uzakluhk* **distance**
uzanmak *uzanmak* **to lie down**
uzman *uzman* **expert**
uzun *uzun* **long**
uzun boylu *uzun boylu* **tall**
uzunluk *uzunluk* **length**
uzuv *uzuv* **organ, limb**

Ü

ücret *ewjret* **fee, salary, wage**
ülke *ewlke* **country**
ünlü *ewnlew* **famous**
üst *ewst* **top**
üst baş *ewst bash* **clothes**
üstünde *ewstewnde* **on top of**
ütü *ewtew* **iron**
ütü yapmak *ewtew yapmak* **to iron**
üzgün *ewzgewn* **sad**
üzülmek *ewzewlmek* **to regret**
üzüm *ewzewm* **grapes**
üzüntü *ewzewntew* **worry, sadness**

V

vadi *va:di* **valley**
vagon *vagon* **carriage**
vagon restoran *vagon restoran* **dining car**
vajina *vazhina* **vagina**
valiz *valiz* **suitcase**
var *var* **there is, are**
varış *varuhsh* **arrival**

varmak *varmak* to arrive
ve *ve* and
vejetaryen *vezhetaryen* vegetarian
vergi *vergi* tax
vermek *vermek* to give
vestiyer *vestiyer* cloakroom
veteriner *veteriner* vet
veya *veya:* or
vida *vida* screw
video *video* video
viraj *virazh* bend (road)
viski *viski* whisky
vitamin *vitamin* vitamins
vize *vize* visa
vurmak *vurmak* to hit
vücut *vewjut* body

Y

ya ... ya *ya ... ya* either ... or
yabancı *yabanjuh* foreign, foreigner,
    imported
yabani *yaba:ni* wild
yağ *ya:* fat, oil
yağlı *ya:luh* greasy
yağmak *ya:mak* to rain
yağmur *ya:mur* rain
    » yağmur yağıyor *ya:mur ya:uhyor* it is
        raining
Yahudi *yahudi* Jewish
yakın *yakuhn* near
yakında *yakuhnda* nearby, soon
yakışmak *yakuhshmak* to suit
yakışıklı *yakuhshuhkluh* handsome
yaklaşık *yaklashuhk* approximately
yanmak *yanmak* to burn
yalan söylemek *yalan söylemek* to lie
yalnız *yalnuhz* alone, only
yan *yan* side
yangın *yanguhn* fire
yangın söndürme cihazı *yanguhn
    söndewrme jihazuh* fire extinguisher
yanık *yanuhk* burn
yanıt *yanuht* answer
yankesici *yankesiji* pickpocket

yanlış *yanluhsh* wrong, mistake
yanmak *yanmak* to get burnt
yapı *yapuh* building
yapı market *yapuh market* DIY shop
yapmak *yapmak* to make, to do
yaprak *yaprak* leaf
yara *yara* wound
yaralamak *yaralamak* to injure
yaralı *yaraluh* injured
yararlı *yararluh* useful
yardım *yarduhm* help
    » yardım etmek *yarduhm etmek* to help
yarım *yaruhm* half
    » yarım pansiyon *yaruhm pansiyon* half
        board
yarın *yaruhn* tomorrow
yasa *yasa* law
yasak *yasak* forbidden, prohibited
yastık *yastuhk* pillow
yaş *yash* age, damp
    » kaç yaşındasınız? *kach
        yashuhndasuhnuhz* how old are you?
yaşam *yasham* life
yaşamak *yashamak* to live
yaşlı *yashluh* old
yat *yat* yacht
yatak *yatak* bed
yatak odası *yatak odasuh* bedroom
yatışmak *yatuhshmak* to calm down
yatmak *yatmak* to go to bed
yavaş *yavash* slow
    » yavaş yavaş *yavash yavash* slowly
yaya *yaya* pedestrian
yaya *yaya* on foot
yazık! *yazuhk* what a pity!
yazmak *yazmak* to write
yedek *yedek* spare, extra
yelken *yelken* sails
yelkenli *yelkenli* sailing boat
yemek listesi *yemek listesi* menu
yemek salonu *yemek salonu* dining room
yemek tarifi *yemek ta:rifi* recipe
yengeç *yengech* crab
yeni *yeni* new

» Yeni Yıl *yeni yuhl* New Year
» Yeni yılınız kutlu olsun *yeni yuhluhnuhz kutlu olsun* Happy New Year
yepyeni *yepyeni* brand new
yer *yer* seat, place, ground
yer ayırtmak *yer ayuhrtmak* to make a reservation
yer fıstığı *yer fuhstuh:uh* peanut
yeşil *yeshil* green
yeter *yeter* enough
yetişkin *yetishkin* adult
yıl *yuhl* year
yılan *yuhlan* snake
Yılbaşı *yuhlbashuh* New Year's Eve
yıldız *yuhlduhz* star
yıllık *yuhlluhk* anniversary
yiyecek *yiyejek* foodstuffs
yok *yok* there isn't, aren't
yoksa *yoksa* otherwise
yolcu *yolju* passenger
yolcu otobüsü *yolju otobewsew* coach
yolculuk *yoljuluk* journey
yorgun *yorgun* tired
yön *yön* direction
yönetici *yönetiji* manager
yukarı *yukaruh* up, upstairs
yumurta *yumurta* egg
yumuşak *yumushak* soft
yurt dışı *yurt duhshuh* abroad, overseas
yutmak *yutmak* to swallow
yuvarlak *yuvarlak* round
yüklemek *yewklemek* to download
yüksek *yewksek* high
yün *yewn* wool
yürümek *yewrewmek* to walk
yürüyüş *yewrewyewsh* walk
yürüyüşe çıkmak *yewrewyewshe chuhkmak* to go for a walk
yüz *yewz* face, a hundred
yüzde *yewzde* per cent
yüzme *yewzme* swimming
yüzmeye gitmek *yewzmeye gitmek* to go swimming

yüzme havuzu *yewzme havuzu* swimming pool
yüzmek *yewzmek* to swim
yüzük *yewzewk* ring
yüzyıl *yewzyuhl* century

Z

zaman *zaman* time
» ne zaman *ne zaman* when
» o zaman *o zaman* then, in that case
zamk *zamk* glue
zarar *zarar* damage, loss
» zarar vermek *zarar vermek* to damage
zarf *zarf* envelope
zarif *zarif* elegant
zavallı! *zavalluh* poor thing!
zayıf *zayuhf* thin, weak
zehir *zehir* poison
zeki *zeki* intelligent, clever
zemin kat *zemin kat* basement
zengin *zengin* rich
zeytin *zeytin* olive
zeytinyağı *zeytinya:uh* olive oil
ziyaret *ziya:ret* visit
» ziyaret etmek *ziya:ret etmek* to visit
zor *zor* difficult

Now you're talking!

BBC Active offers a wide range of innovative resources, from short courses and grammars, to more in-depth courses for beginners or intermediates. Designed by language-teaching experts, our courses make the best use of today's technology, with book and audio, audio-only and multi-media products on offer. Many of these courses are accompanied by free online activities and television series, which are regularly repeated on BBC TWO Learning Zone.

Independent, interactive study course
CD-ROM; 144pp course book;
60-min audio CD; free online activities
and resources www.getinto.com.

Travel pack
160pp book;
1 x 75-minute
CD.

Short independent
study course
128pp book;
2 x 60-minute CDs/
cassettes.